Stories & Poems by Elizabeth Stuart Phelps

Elizabeth Stuart Phelps Ward was born in Andover, Massachusetts on August 31st 1844 and baptized as Mary Gray Phelps. Her mother was ill for most of her adult life and died of brain fever shortly after the birth of her third child on November 20, 1852. Eight year old Mary Gray asked to be renamed in honor of her mother

Elizabeth attended the very well to do Abbot Academy and Mrs. Edwards' School for Young Ladies where her gift for telling stories was first noticed. By thirteen she had been published in Youth's Companion and other had appeared in Sunday School publications.

At age 19 she sent a Civil War story "A Sacrifice Consumed" to Harper's Magazine. The editor sent her a generous payment and asked her to write for them again. In 1864 Harpers published her first adult fiction. Elizabeth then began writing her first books for children; the "Tiny series" followed by the four-volume Gypsy Brenton series.

The Atlantic Monthly published her story "The Tenth of January" in March 1868 about the death of scores of girls in the Pemberton Mill collapse and fire in Lawrence, Massachusetts on January 10, 1860. Also in 1868, came The Gates Ajar, in which the afterlife was a place with all the comforts of domestic life and reunited families – and their pets – for all eternity.

She wrote realistic adventures based on a four-year old boy named Trotty, The Trotty Book (1870) and Trotty's Wedding Tour, and Story-book (1873).

In her 40s, Elizabeth married a man 17 years her junior, another step in her unconventional stands. Years later she urged women to burn their corsets! Her later writing focused on feminine ideals and women's financial dependence on men in marriage.

In 1876 she became the first woman to present a lecture series at Boston University entitled "Representative Modern Fiction."

In 1877 she published a novel, The Story of Avis, that was ahead of its time. The work centers on many of the early feminist issues of her era. In it she portrayed a woman's struggle to balance her married life and domestic duties with her desire to become a painter.

With her husband she co-authored two Biblical romances in 1890 and 1891.

Her autobiography, Chapters from a Life was published in 1896 after being serialized in McClure's.

Her novel, Trixy, published in 1904, was constructed around the topic of vivisection and the effect this kind of training had on doctors. The book became a standard polemic against experimentation on animals.

During her lifetime she was the author of 57 volumes of fiction, poetry and essays. In many she challenged society's view of women and placed them as women succeeding in careers as physicians, ministers, and artists.

Elizabeth Stuart Phelps Ward died January 28, 1911, in Newton Center, Massachusetts.

Index Of Contents

A CHARIOT OF FIRE

When the White Mountain express to Boston stopped at Beverly, it slowed down reluctantly, crashed off the baggage, and dashed on with the nervousness of a train that is unmercifully and unpardonably late.

It was a September night, and the channel of home-bound summer travel was clogged and heaving.

A middle-aged man, a plain fellow, who was one of the Beverly passengers, stood for a moment staring at the tracks. The danger-light from the rear of the onrushing train wavered before his eyes, and looked like a splash of blood that was slowly wiped out by the night. It was foggy, and the atmosphere clung like a sponge.

"No," he muttered, "it's the other way. Batty's the other way."

He turned, facing towards the branch road which carries the great current of North Shore life.

"How soon can I get to Gloucester?" he demanded of one who brushed against him heavily. He who answered proved to be of the baggage staff, and was at that moment skilfully combining a frown and a whistle behind a towering truck; from this two trunks and a dress-suit case threatened to tumble on a bull-terrier leashed to something invisible, and yelping in the darkness behind.

"Lord! This makes 'leven dogs, cats to burn, twenty-one baby-carriages, and a guinea-pig travellin' over this blamed road since yesterday. What's that? Gloucester? 6.45 to-morrow morning."

"Oh, but look here!" cried the plain passenger, "that won't do. I have got to get to Gloucester to-night."

"So's this bull-terrier," groaned the baggage-handler. "He got switched off without his folks, and I've got a pet lamb in the baggage-room bleatin' at the corporation since dinner-time. Some galoot forgot the crittur. There's a lost parrot settin' alongside that swears in several foreign languages. I wish to Moses I could!"

The passenger experienced the dull surprise of one in acute calamity who wonders that another man can jest. He turned without remark, and went to the waiting-room; he limped a little, for he was slightly lame. The ticket-master was locking the door of the office, and looked sleepy and fagged.

"Where's the train to Gloucester?"

"Gone."

"'Tain't gone?"

"Gone half an hour ago."

The official pointed to the clock, on whose face an ominous expression seemed to rest, and whose hands marked the hour of half-past twelve.

"But I have got to get to Gloucester!" answered the White Mountain passenger. "We had an accident. We're late. I ain't much used to travellin', I supposed they'd wait for us. I tell you I've got to get there!"

In his agitation he gripped the arm of the other, who threw the grasp off instinctively.

"You'll have to walk, then. You can't get anything now till the newspaper train."

"God!" gasped the belated passenger. "I've got a little boy. He's dying."

"Sho!" said the ticket-master. "That's too bad. Can you afford a team? You might try the stables. There's one or two around here."

The ticket-master locked the doors of the station and walked away, but did not go far. A humane uneasiness disturbed him, and he returned to see if he could be of any use to the afflicted passenger.

"I'll show you the way to the nearest," he began, kindly.

But the man had gone.

In the now dimly lighted town square he was, in fact, zigzagging about alone, with the loping gait of a lame man in a feverish hurry.

"There must be hosses," he muttered, "and places. Why, yes. Here's one, first thing."

Into the livery-stable he entered so heavily that he seemed to fall in. His cheap straw hat was pushed back from his head; he was flushed, and his eyes were too bright; his hair, which was red and coarse, lay matted on his forehead.

"I want a team," he began, on a high, sharp key. "I've got to get to Gloucester. The train's gone."

A sleepy groom, who scowled at him, turned on a suspicious heel. "You're drunk. It's fourteen miles. It would cost you more'n you're worth."

"I've got a little boy," repeated the lame man. "He's dying."

The groom wheeled back. "That so? Why, that's a pity. I'd like to 'commodate you. See? I'm here alone, see? I darsen't go so far without orders. Boss is home and abed."

"He got hurt in an accident," pleaded the father. "I come from up to Conway. I went to bury my uncle. They sent me a telegraph about my little boy. I ain't drunk. They sent me the telegraph. I've got to get home."

"I'll let you sleep here along of me," suggested the groom, "but I daresn't leave. I'm responsible to the boss. There's other places you might get one. I'll show you. See? I'd try 'em all if I was you."

But again the man was gone.

By the time he had found another stable his manner had changed; he had become deprecating, servile. He entreated, he trembled; he flung his emergency at the feet of the watchman; he reiterated his phrase:

"I've got a little boy, if you please. He's dying. I've got to get to Gloucester, I live in Squam."

"I don't like to refuse you," protested the night-watchman, "but two of my horses are lame, and one is plumb used up carrying summer folks. I'm dreadful short. I haven't a team to my name I could put on the road to Gloucester. It's, why, to Squam it's seventeen miles, thirty-four the round trip. It would cost you -"

"I'll pay!" cried the lame man; "I'll pay. I ain't beggin'."

"I'm sorry I haven't got a horse," apologized the watchman. "It would cost you ten dollars if I had. But I hain't."

"Ten dollars?" The traveller echoed the words stupidly.

"I'm sorry; fact, I am," urged the watchman. "Won't you set 'n' rest a spell?"

But the visitor had vanished from the office.

Twenty minutes after, the door-bell of a home in the old residence portion of the town rang violently and pealed through the sleeping house.

It was a comfortable, not a new-fashioned, house, sometimes leased to summer citizens, and modernized in a measure for their convenience; one of the few of its kind within reach of the station, and by no means near.

When the master of the family had turned on all the burglar electricity and could get the screen up, he put his head out of the window, and so perceived on his door-step a huddled figure with a white, uplifted face.

A shaking voice came up:

"Sir? Be you a gentleman?"

"I hope so," went down the quiet reply. "But I can't remember that I was ever asked that question at this time of morning before."

"Be you a Christian?" insisted the voice from below.

"Sometimes, perhaps," went down the voice from above.

The voice from below came up: "Sir! Sir! I'm in great trouble. For the love of Christ, sir, come down, quick!"

"Why, of course," said the voice from above.

The man stood quite still when the great bolts of the door shot through their grooves. Against a background of electric brilliance he saw a gentleman in pajamas and bathrobe, with slippers as soft as a lady's on his white feet. The face of the gentleman was somewhat fixed and guarded; his features were carefully cut, behind their heavy coat of seaside tan.

"Well," he said, "that was a pretty solemn adjuration. What is it?"

"I want to get a team," stammered the figure on the steps. Suddenly, somehow, his courage had begun to falter. He felt the enormity of his intrusion. He came up against the mystery of social distinctions; his great human emergency seemed to be distanced by the little thing men call difference of class.

"You want to get a team?" repeated the gentleman; he spoke slowly, without irritation. "You have made a mistake. This is not a livery-stable."

"Livery-stable!" cried the intruder, with a swift and painful passion. "I've tried three! Fust one hadn't any boss. Next one hadn't any hoss. It was ten dollars if he had. Last one wanted 'leven dollars, pay in advance. I've got four dollars 'n' sixteen cents in my pocket. I've been up to Conway to bury my uncle. My folks sent me a telegraph. My little boy, he's had an accident. My train was late. I've got to get to Gloucester, sir. So I thought," added the traveller, simply, "I'd ask one of the neighbors. Neighbors is most gener'lly kind. Up our way they be. Sir, could you let me have a team to see my little boy before, in case, he dies?"

"Come inside a minute," replied the gentleman.

The words, which had began shortly, ended softly. "Perfectly sober," he thought. His fingers stole to the button of a bell as the stranger stepped into the hall.

"Yes, I'll send you over. What's your name?"

"Dryver, sir. Jacob Dryver."

"Where do you live?"

"Squam."

"Annisquam? That is several miles beyond Gloucester. Your trouble is too swift for horses. I have rung for my chauffeur. I'll send you in the automobile. Be so good as to step around to the stables, Mr. Dryver. I'll join you outside."

Now the voice of a sleepy child could be heard overhead; it seemed to be trying to say "Popper! Popper!" A woman's figure drifted to the top of the padded stairs. The intruder caught a gleam of delicate white drapery floating with laces, closely gathered at the throat, and held with one ringed hand, as if it had been hastily thrown on. The door shut, and the bolts shot again. Jacob Dryver felt that he was at once trusted and distrusted; he could not have said why he did not go to the stables, but sat down on the broad granite steps. His knees hung apart; his elbows dropped to them; his face fell into his hands.

The child above continued to call: "Popper! Popper!" Then the little voice trailed away.

"It's smaller 'n Batty," Jacob said.

When he lifted his head from his hands, up the curving avenue an automobile was sweeping upon him. Its acetylene lanterns blazed like the eyes of some prehistoric thing; but this simple fellow knew nothing about prehistoric things. The lanterns reminded him of the living creatures that Ezekiel saw. Such imagination as he had was Biblically trained, and leaped from Ezekiel to Elijah easily.

"It's a chariot of fire," thought Jacob Dryver, "comin' for to carry me home."

As he gathered himself and went to meet the miracle, a dark figure, encased in rubber armor from foot to head, brought the carriage to a swift and artistic stop.

"Are you the shove-her?" asked Jacob, timidly.

"I am not the shove-her," replied the figure at the brake, "and I hope I sha'n't have to be. I am Mr. Chester. My chauffeur is not at home, I find. I shall drive you to Annisquam myself."

"You're takin' some trouble, sir," said Jacob, slowly. His head reeled. He felt that he was growing stupid under the whirlwind of events. He went down the long steps like a lame blind man. As he did so the bolts of the door behind him leaped back again, and the lady ran down and slid into the automobile. The fog glittered on the laces of her white woollen garment. Her husband thought of it as a negligée, but Jacob called it a wrapper. She was a dainty lady, and fair to look upon; her hair lay in long, bright braids upon her shoulders; she had caught up an automobile coat and cap, which she flung across her arm. Dryver heard her say: "I shall be a little anxious. After all, you know nothing about him. Mayn't I go?"

"And leave Bert? I don't think I would, Mary. I've told James to sit up and watch. Draw the big bolt on top, and keep the lights all on. If I have good luck I shall be back in less than two hours. Good-bye, Mary, dear."

The last word lingered with the caressing accent which only long-tried marriage love ever puts into it. The lips of the two met silently, and, drooping, the lady melted away. Jacob Dryver found himself in the automobile, speeding down the avenue to the silent street. He looked back once at the house. Every pane of glass was blazing as if the building were on fire.

"You'll find it colder than you expect," observed Mr. Chester. "I brought along Thomas's coat. Put it on, and hold on. Never in one of these before, were you?"

"N-no, sir," chattered Jacob Dryver. "Thank you, sir. I n-never was."

He clung to the side of the seat desperately. In fact, he was very much frightened. But he would have gone under the heavy wheels before he would have owned it. Spinning through the deserted Beverly streets the automobile took what seemed to him a startling pace.

"I'm going slowly till we get out of town," remarked Mr. Chester. "Once on the Manchester road I'll let her out a bit."

Jacob made no reply. What had seemed to be fog drenched and drowned him now like driving rain. There had been no wind, but now the powers and principalities of the air were let loose. He gasped for breath, which was driven down his throat. That made him think of Batty, whom, for the moment, he had actually forgotten. When people died, they could not, Had Batty, by this time, it was so long, should he find that Batty -

"What ails your boy?" asked the half-invisible figure from the depths of its rubber armor.

"I had a telegraph," said Jacob, monotonously. "I never was away from home so far, I ain't used to travellin'. I supposed the train would wait for the accident. The telegraph said he was hurt bad. I got it just as the fun'ril was leavin' the house. I had to quit it, corpse 'n' all for Batty. I ran all the way to the depot. I just got aboard, and here I be becalmed all night, and there is Batty. His name is Batwing," added the father. "He was named after the uncle I went to bury. But we call him Batty."

"Any more children?" inquired Mr. Chester, in the cultivated, compassionate voice which at once attracted and estranged the breaking heart of Jacob Dryver.

"We haven't only Batty, sir," he choked.

The hand on the lever tightened; the throttle opened; the dark figure in the rubber coat bent, and its muscles turned to iron. The automobile began to rock and fly. It was now whirling out upon the silent, sleeping road that goes by the great houses of the North Shore.

"I'll let her out a little," said Mr. Chester, quietly. "Don't worry. We'll get there before you know it."

The car took on a considerable pace. Jacob's best straw hat flew off, but he did not mention it. His red hair stood endwise, all ways, on his head; his eyes started; his hands gripped, one at the rail, one at the knee of his companion. The wind raised by the motion of the car became a gale and forced itself into his lungs. Jacob gasped:

"It's on account of Batty."

"I have a little boy of my own," observed Mr. Chester. Plainly thinking to divert the attention of the anguished father, he continued: "He had an accident this summer, he was hurt by a scythe; he slipped away from his nurse. He was pretty badly hurt. I was away, I hurried from Bar Harbor to get to him. I think I know how you feel."

"Did you have a telegraph, sir?" asked Dryver, rousing to the throb of the common human poise.

"Yes, there was a telegram. But I was a good while getting it. I understand your position."

"Did he ever get over it, your little boy? Oh, I see; that was him I heard. 'Popper,' he says, 'Popper.'"

Above the whir of the automobile, above the chatter of the exhaust, above the voice of the wind, the sound of a man's muffled groan came distinctly to the ear that was fine enough to hear it.

"Trust me," said Chester, gently. "I'll get you there. I'll get you to your boy."

The gentleman's face was almost as white now as Jacob Dryver's. The fog glistened upon his mustache and made him look a gray-haired man, as he emerged from gulfs of darkness and shot by widely scattered dim street lamps. Both men had acquired something of the same expression, the rude face and the finished one; both wore the solemn, elemental look of fatherhood.

The heart of one repeated piteously: "It's Batty."

But the other thought: "What if it were Bert?"

"I'll let her out a little more," repeated Chester. The car throbbed and rocked to the words.

"How do you like my machine?" he added, in a comfortable voice. He felt that the mercury of emotion had mounted too far. "Mrs. Chester has named her," he proceeded. "We call her Aurora."

"Hey?"

"We've named the machine Aurora, I said."

"'Roarer,' sir?"

"Oh, well, that will do - 'Roarer,' if you like. That isn't bad. It's an improvement, perhaps. By-the-way, how did you happen on my place to-night? There are a good many nearer the station; you had quite a walk."

"I see a little pair o' reins an' bells in the grass alongside, such as little boys play horse with. We had one once for Batty, sir."

"Ah! Was that it? What's your business, Dryver? You haven't told me. Do you fish?"

"Winters, I make paving-stones. Summers, I raise vegetables," replied Jacob Dryver. "I'm a kind of a quarry-farmer. My woman she plants flowers for the summer folks, and Batty bunches 'em up and delivers 'em. Batty, he, God! My God! Mebbe there ain't any Batty -"

The sentence broke. In truth, it would have been hard to find its remnants in the sudden onset of sound made by the motion of the machine.

The car was freed now to the limit of her mighty strength. She took great leaps like those of a living heart that is overexcited. Powerfully, perfectly, without let or hindrance, without flaw or accident, the chariot of fire bounded through the night. A trail of smoke like the tail of a comet followed her. The dark scenery of the guarded shore flew by; Montserrat was behind; Prides' was gone; the Farms blew past.

They were now well out upon the beautiful, silent Manchester road, where the woods, solemn at noonday, are sinister at dead of night. The automobile, flying through them, encountered no answering sign of life. Both men had ceased to speak. Awe fell upon them, as if in the presence of more than natural things. Once it seemed to Dryver as if he saw a boy running beside the machine, a little fellow, white, like a spirit, and, like a spirit, silent. Chester's hands had stiffened to the throttle; his face had the stern rigidity of those on whom life or human souls absolutely depend. Neither man spoke now aloud.

To himself Jacob Dryver repeated: "It's Batty! It's my Batty!"

And Hurlburt Chester thought: "What if it were Bert?"

Now the great arms of the sea began to open visibly before them. The fog on their lips grew salter, and they seemed to have entered the Cave of the Winds. Slender beach and sturdy headland slid by. West Manchester, Manchester, Magnolia rushed past. In the Magnolia woods they lost the sea again; but the bell-buoy called from Norman's Woe, and they could hear the moan of the whistling-buoy off Eastern Point. In the Cape Ann Light the fog bell was tolling.

At the pace which the car was taking there was an element of danger in the situation which Jacob Dryver could not measure, since he feared safety ignorantly and met peril with composure. Chester reduced the speed a little, and yet a little more, but pushed on steadily. Once Jacob spoke.

"I'll bet your shove-her couldn't drive like you do," he said, proudly.

Fresh Water Cove slipped by; Old Stage Fort was behind; the Aurora bumped over the pavement of the Cut, and reeled through the rough and narrow streets of Gloucester. He of Beverly was familiar with the route, and asked no questions. The car, now tangled among electric tracks, swung around the angle from Main Street carefully, jarred across the railroad, and took the winding, dim road to Annisquam.

Bay View flew behind, the bridge, the village, the pretty arcade known as Squam Willows. The automobile dashed into it and out of it as if it were a tunnel. Then Dryver gripped the other's arm and, without a word, pointed.

The car followed the guidance of his shaking finger, and, like a conscious creature, swung to a startling stop.

There were lights in the quarryman's cottage, and shadows stirred against drawn shades. Jacob Dryver tumbled out and ran. He did not speak, nor by a gesture thank his Beverly "neighbor." Chester slowly unbuttoned his rubber coat and got at his watch. The Aurora had covered the distance, in dark and fog, over seventeen miles, in fifty-six minutes. Now, Jacob, dashing in, had left the door open, and Chester, as he put his watch back into its pocket, heard that which sent the blood driving through his arteries as the power had driven the pumps of the car. The sound that he heard was the fretful moan of a hurt child.

As he had admitted, he was a Christian, sometimes; and he said, "Oh, thank God!" with all his generous heart. Indeed, as he did so, he took off his heavy cap and bared his head.

Then he heard the sobbing of a shaken man close beside him.

"Sir! Oh, sir! The God of Everlastin' bless you, sir. Won't you come and look at him?"

Batty lay quietly; he had put his little fingers in his father's hand; he did not notice the stranger. The boy's mother, painfully poised on one elbow in the position that mothers take when they watch sick children, lay upon the other side of the bed. She was a large woman, with a plain, good face. She had on a polka-dotted, blue cotton wrapper which nobody called a negligée. Her mute, maternal eyes went to the face of the visitor and reverted to the child.

There was a physician in the room, a very young, to the trained eye an inexperienced, man; in fact, the medical situation was unpromising and complicated. It took Chester but a few moments to gauge it, and to perceive that his mission to this afflicted household had not ended with a lost night's sleep and an automobile record.

The local doctor, it seemed, was away from home when Batty's accident befell; the Gloucester surgeon was ill; some one had proposed the hospital, but the mother had the prejudices of her class. A neighbor had suggested this young man, a new-comer to the town, one of the flotsam practitioners who drift and disappear. Recommended upon the ground that he had successfully prescribed headache pills to a Swedish cook, this stranger had received into his unskilled hands the emergency of a dangerously wounded lad. The accident, in fact, was more serious than Chester had supposed. He had now been told that the child was crushed by an automobile racing through Annisquam Willows the day before.

The boy, it was plain, was sorely hurt, and ignorant suffering lay at the mercy of ignorant treatment, in the hopeless and helpless subjection to medical etiquette which costs so many lives.

"Dryver," said Chester, quietly, "you need a surgeon here at once. Your physician is quite willing to consult with any one you may call." He shot one stern glance at the young doctor, who quavered a frightened assent. "I know a distinguished surgeon, he is a friend of mine; it was he who saved my boy in that accident I told you of, this summer. He is not far away; he is at a hotel on Eastern Point. I can have him here in twenty, well, say twenty-five minutes. Of course, we must wait for him to dress."

The woman raised her head and stared upon the gentleman. One swift, brilliant gleam shot from her heavy eyes. She had read of angels in the Bible. She had noticed, indeed, that they were men angels. But she had never heard of one in a rubber touring-coat, drenched from head to foot with fog, spattered from foot to head with mud, and with a wedding-ring upon his fine hand.

Jacob Dryver began: "Sir! The God of Everlastin' - " but he sobbed so that he could not finish what he would have said. So Chester went out and oiled the Aurora, opened the throttle, and started off again, and dashed through the rude streets of Gloucester to her summer shore.

Dawn was rose-gray over Eastern Point, and the tide had turned upon the harbor, when the "Roarer" curved up quietly to the piazza of the hotel.

It was rose-gray upon Annisquam, and the tide was rising up the river, when the great surgeon went into the little place where the lad lay fighting for his mangled life. There had been some delay in rousing the sleeper, it was a trip of six rough miles twice taken, and it was thirty-five minutes before his "merciless merciful" hands went to work upon the mortal need of the boy.

The child had been crushed across the hips and body, and only an experienced or only an eminent skill could have saved the little fellow.

In the blossoming day Jacob Dryver limped out and stood in the front yard among his wife's flowers that Batty "bunched up" and sold to summer people. He could not perceive the scent of the flowers, only that of the ether. His big boot caught in a sweet-pea vine and tore it. One of the famous carmine dahlias of Cape Ann seemed to turn its large face and gaze at him.

An old neighbor, a cross-eyed lobsterer, going to his traps, came by, cast a shrewd look, and asked how the boy was. Jacob did not reply to the lobsterer; he lifted his wet eyes to the sky, then they fell to a bed of blazing nasturtiums, which seemed to smoke before them. His lips tried to form the words which close like a strangling hand upon the throat of the poor in all the emergencies of life. Till he has answered this question a poor man may not love a woman or rear a child; he may not bury his dead or save his living.

"What will it cost?" asked Jacob Dryver. He looked piteously at the great surgeon, whose lips parted to speak. But Hurlburt Chester raised an imperious hand.

"That," he said, "is my affair."

It was broad, bright day when the Aurora came whirring home. Chester nodded to his wife at the window, but went directly to the stables. It was a little longer than she expected before he returned. She waited at the head of the stairs, then hurried half-way down to meet him. Her white robe was ungirdled and flowing; it fell apart, the laces above from the laces below, and the tired man's kiss fell upon her soft throat.

She was naturally a worrier in a sweet-natured way, but he had always been patient with her little weakness; some men are, with anxious women.

"No," he smiled, but rather feebly; "you've missed it again. The boy is saved. St. Clair's got hold of him. I'll talk presently, Mary, not just now."

In fact, he would say no more till he had bathed and taken food. He looked so exhausted that she brought his breakfast to his bed, serving it with her own hands, and asking no questions at all; for, although she worried, she was wise. She sent for the baby, too, a big baby, three years old, and Chester enfolded the chin of the child in his slender brown hand silently.

Then he said: "Lock the door, Mary. I've something to tell you."

When she had drawn the brass bolt and returned, somewhat pale herself with wonder and alarm, to the side of the bed, her husband spoke abruptly:

"Mary, you've got to know it, may as well have it over. I found this pinned on the stable wall. It was the Aurora that ran over the - that - that poor little fellow."

His hand shook as he laid the piece of paper in her own. And while she read it he covered his face; for he was greatly over-worn, and the strain which he had undergone seemed now to have leaped again with the spring of a creature that one supposes one has left lifeless behind.

Mrs. Chester read the writing and laid it down. It ran like this:

MR. CHESTER:

Sir, Ime goin away while I can. It was me run over that boy while you was in town. I took Her out for a spin. I let Her out some racin with another one in the Willows an he got under Her someways. I see it in the papers so I was afraid of manslorter. Ime awful cut up about it so Ime goin to lite out while I can.

Your obedient servant,
THOMAS.

The eyes of the husband and wife met silently. She was the first to speak.

"Do they know?"

Chester shook his head.

"You'll tell them, of course?"

"I haven't made up my mind."

The baby was jabbering loudly on the bed, he was very noisy; it was not easy for her to hear what was said.

"I'm sure you ought to tell them!" she cried, passionately.

"Perhaps so. But I'd like to think it over."

A subtle terror slid over her face. "What can they do to you? I don't know about such things. Is there any law?"

"Laws enough, laws in plenty. But I'm not answerable for the crimes of my chauffeur. It's only a question of damages."

The wife of the rich man drew a long breath. "Oh, if it's nothing but money!"

"Not that it would make any difference if they could touch me," he continued, with a proud motion of his tired head. "It's purely a question of feeling, it's a question of right within a right, Mary. It's to do what is really kind by these people. Why, Mary, if you could have seen it! From beginning to end it was the most beautiful, the most wonderful thing. Nothing of the kind ever happened to me before. Mary, if an angel from the throne of God had done it, they couldn't have felt, they couldn't have treated me, it was enough to make a fellow a better man the rest of his days. Why, it was worth living for, I tell you! ... And now to let them know..."

Hurlburt Chester was very tired, as we say. He choked, and hid his pale face in his pillow. And his wife laid hers beside it and cried, as women do, without pretending that she didn't. But the baby laughed aloud. And then there drove through the father's mind the repeated phrase which followed the race of the "Roarer" all the way from Beverly to Annisquam:

"What if it were Bert?"

Chester's head whirled yet from the fatigue and jar of the trip, and the words seemed to take leaps through his brain as the car leaped when she was at the top of her great speed. So he kissed the child, and dashed a drop from his cheek quite openly, since only Mary saw.

A constraint unusual to their candid relations breathed like a fog between the husband and the wife; indeed, it did not lift altogether as the autumn opened and closed.

Chester's visits to Annisquam (in which she once or twice accompanied him) were many and merciful; and the distinguished surgeon took the responsibility of the case till the boy was quite convalescent. The lad recovered slowly, but St. Clair promised that the cure would be complete.

The touching gratitude of Jacob Dryver amounted to an idealization such as the comfortable, undramatic life of Chester had never experienced. He seemed to swim in it as an imaginative person dreams of swimming in the air, tree-high above the heads of the crowd on the earth. The situation had become to him a fine intoxicant, but it had its reactions, as intoxicants must.

September and October burned to ashes upon the North Shore. Fire of maple, flash of sumac, torch of elder, flare of ivy, faded into brown November, and the breakers off the Beverly coast took on the greens and blues of north-wind weather below the line of silver surf.

The Chesters closed "their own hired house" and moved to town. The Aurora remained in her stable, nor had she left it since the morning when she came wearily back from Annisquam.

His wife had noticed, but had not seemed to notice, that Chester rode no more that fall. She noted too, but did not seem to note, that he continued his visits to the injured lad after they had returned to the city.

On all the great holidays he made a point of going down, Thanksgiving, Christmas, and New-Year's Day. Mrs. Chester had wished to duplicate for the quarryman's boy the Christmas gifts of her own child (such had been her pretty fancy), but Batty was quite a lad, ten years old; and Bert, like a spoiled collie, was yet a baby, and likely to remain so for some time to come. So the mother contented herself, perforce, with less intimate remembrances. Once, when she had packed a box of miracles, toys and books, clothes and candy, she thrust it from her with a cry: "They would never touch these, if they knew! Hurlburt! Hurlburt! don't you think they ought to know?"

"Do what you think best, Mary," he said, wearily. "I have never been able to decide that question. But you are free to do so if you prefer."

He regarded her with an expression that went to her heart. She flung herself into his arms and tried to kiss it away.

Now, Mary Chester, as we have said, was a worrier, and the worrier never lets a subject go. As the winter set in, her mind closed about the matter which had troubled her, and it began to become unbearable, like a foreign substance in the flesh.

On a January afternoon, it was one of those dark days when souls cloud over, she flung on her furs, and leaving a pencilled line to her husband saying what she had done, she took the train to Gloucester, and a dreary electric-car to Annisquam.

The flowers in the front yard were knee-deep in snow, and Batty sat in the window busy with a Sorrento wood-saw of her providing. He laughed outright when he saw her, and his mother flung open the door as if she had flung open her heart.

"Land!" she cried. "In all this snow!"

She finished tying a fresh white apron over her polka-dotted blue wrapper, and joyously led the lady in.

Batty was a freckled little fellow, with red hair like his father's; he had the pretty imperiousness of a sick and only child who has by all the sorceries contrived to escape petulance. When he had greeted the visitor, he ran back to his jig-saw. He was carving camwood, which stained his fingers crimson.

"I want to see you, alone," began Mrs. Chester, nervously. It had been one of Chester's pleasures to warm the entire house for the convalescent lad, and big coal fires were purring in Batty's bedroom and in the ten-foot "parlor," whither his mother conducted her guest. The doors were left open. The scent of the camwood came across, pungent and sickening. The fret of the jig-saw went on steadily.

"He's makin' a paper-cutter, for Mr. Chester," observed Batty's mother. "He made a watch-case last week, for Mr. Chester."

Mary Chester paled, and she plunged at once:

"There's something I've come to tell, I've got to tell you. We can't keep it to ourselves any longer. I have come to tell you how it happened - that Batty - We thought you'd rather not know -"

"Lord! my dear," said the quarryman's wife, "we've known it all the while."

The visitor's head swam. She laid it down upon her gloved hands on Mrs. Dryver's centre-table. This had a marble top, and felt as the quarries look in winter on Cape Ann. What were tears that they should warm it? The sound of the jig-saw grew uneven and stopped.

"Hush!" said the boy's mother. "Batty don't know; he's the only one that don't."

She tiptoed and shut the doors.

"You never seen Peter Trawl, did you? He's a neighbor, cross-eyed, sells lobsters, well, it was him picked Batty up to the Willows that day. So he seen the number runnin' away, an' so he told. We've known it from fust to last, my dear."

"And never spoke!" said Mary Chester. "And never spoke!"

"What's the use of jabberin'?" asked Batty's mother. "We thought Mr. Chester 'd feel so bad," she added. "We thought he didn't know."

The worrier began to laugh, then cry, first this, then that; for her nerves gave way beneath her. She sat humbly in her rich furs before the quarryman's wife. She felt that these plain people had outdone her in nobility, as they had rivalled her in delicacy, her, and Hurlburt, too.

"Oh, come and see my baby!" she cried. It was the only thing that occurred to her to say.

Now at that moment Batty gave a little yelp of ecstasy, threw down his jig-saw, and got to the front door. His father was there, stamping off the snow, and the lad's idol, his ideal, his man angel, stood upon the threshold, nervous, for an angel, and with an anxious look.

But when the two men saw the women crying together upon the quarry-cold centre-table, they clasped hands and said nothing at all.

SONGS OF THE SILENT WORLD & OTHER POEMS

Dear! Is the distance vast? I cross it here.
The chasm fathomless? I span it thus.
The silence dread? I break it. What is fear?
When only our own hearts can sever us.

The gold and frankincense I should have given,
Envy the myrrh I lay within your hand;
Dearer to me than fame of earth or heaven
It is, to know that you will understand.

Contents

SONGS OF THE SILENT WORLD.

AFTERWARD.

There is no vacant chair. The loving meet
A group unbroken, smitten, who knows how?
One sitteth silent only, in his usual seat;
We gave him once that freedom. Why not now?

Perhaps he is too weary, and needs rest;
He needed it too often, nor could we
Bestow. God gave it, knowing how to do so best.
Which of us would disturb him? Let him be.

There is no vacant chair. If he will take
The mood to listen mutely, be it done.
By his least mood we crossed, for which the heart must ache,
Plead not nor question! Let him have this one.

Death is a mood of life. It is no whim
By which life's Giver mocks a broken heart.
Death is life's reticence. Still audible to Him,
The hushed voice, happy, speaketh on, apart.

There is no vacant chair. To love is still
To have. Nearer to memory than to eye,
And dearer yet to anguish than to comfort, will
We hold him by our love, that shall not die.

For while it doth not, thus he cannot. Try!
Who can put out the motion or the smile?
The old ways of being noble all with him laid by?
Because we love, he is. Then trust awhile.

RELEASED.

Oh, joy of the dying!
At last thou art mine.
And leaping to meet thee,
Impatient to greet thee,
A rapid and rapturous, sensitive, fine
Gayety steals through my pulses to-day,
Daring and doubting like pleasure
Forbidden, or Winter looking at May.

Oh, sorrow of living!
Make way for the thrill
Of the soul that is starting
Onlooking, departing

Across the threshold of clay.
Bend, bow to the will
Of the soul that is up and away!

THE ROOM'S WIDTH.

I think if I should cross the room,
Far as fear;
Should stand beside you like a thought
Touch you, Dear!

Like a fancy. To your sad heart
It would seem
That my vision passed and prayed you,
Or my dream.

Then you would look with lonely eyes
Lift your head
And you would stir, and sigh, and say
"She is dead."

Baffled by death and love, I lean
Through the gloom.
O Lord of life! am I forbid
To cross the room?

THE FIRST CHRISTMAS APART.

The shadows watch about the house;
Silent as they, I come.
Oh, it is true that life is deaf,
And not that death is dumb.

The Christmas thrill is on the earth,
The stars throb in the sky.
Love listens in a thousand homes,
The Christmas bells ring by.

I cross the old familiar door
And take the dear old chair.
You look with desolated eyes
Upon me sitting there.

You gaze and see not, though the tears
In gazing burn and start.
Believe, the living are the blind,
Not that the dead depart.

A year ago some words we said

Kept sacred 'twixt us twain,
'T is you, poor Love, who answer not,
The while I speak again.

I lean above you as before,
Faithful, my arms enfold.
Oh, could you know that life is numb,
Nor think that death is cold!

Senses of earth, how weak ye are!
Joys, joys of Heaven how strong!
Loves of the earth, how short and sad,
Of Heaven how glad and long!

Heart of my heart! if earth or Heaven
Had speech or language fine
Enough, or death or life could give
Me symbol, sound, or sign

To reach you, thought, or touch, or eye,
Body or soul, I 'd die
Again, to make you understand:
My darling! This is I!

THE ANGEL JOY.

Oh, was it a death-dream not dreamed through,
That eyed her like a foe?
Or only a sorrow left over from life,
Half-finished years ago?

How long was it since she died, who told?
Or yet what was death, who knew?
She said: "I am come to Heaven at last,
And I'll do as the blessed do."

But the custom of earth was stronger than Heaven,
And the habit of life than death,
How should an anguish as old as thought
Be healed by the end of breath?

Tissue and nerve and pulse of her soul
Had absorbed the disease of woe.
The strangest of all the angels there
Was Joy. (Oh, the wretched know!)

"I am too tired with earth," she said,
"To rest me in Paradise.
Give me a spot to creep away,
And close my heavy eyes.

"I must learn to be happy in Heaven," she said,
"As we learned to suffer below."
"Our ways are not your ways," he said,
"And ours the ways you go."

As love, too wise for a word, puts by
All a woman's weak alarms,
Joy hushed her lips, and gathered her
Into his mighty arms.

He took her to his holy heart,
And there, for he held her fast
The saddest spirit in the world,
Came to herself at last.

"ABSENT!"[1]
You do not lift your eyes to watch
Us pass the conscious door;
Your startled ear perceiveth not
Our footfall on the floor;
No eager word your lips betray
To greet us when we stand;
We throng to meet you, but you hold
To us no beckoning hand.

Faint as the years in which we breathed,
Far as the death we died,
Dim as the faded battle-smoke,
We wander at your side;
Cold as a cause outlived, or lost,
Vague as the legends told
At twilight, of a mystic band
Circling an Age of Gold.

Unseen, unheard, unfelt, and yet,
Beneath the army blue
Our heart-beats sounded real enough
When we were boys like you.
We turned us from your fabled lore,
With ancient passion rife;
No myth, our solemn laying down
Of love, and hope, and life.

No myth, the clasped and severed hands,
No dream, the last replies.
Upon the desolated home
To-day, the sunlight lies.
Take, sons of peace, your heritage

Our loss, your legacy;
Our action be your fables fair,
Our facts, your poetry.

O ye who fall on calmer times!
The perils of the calm
Are yours, the swell, the sloth, the sleep,
The carelessness of harm,
The keel that rides the gale, to strike
Where the warm waves are still;
Ours were the surf, the stir, the shock,
The tempest and the thrill.

Comrades, be yours that vigor old,
Be yours the elected power
That fits a man, like rock to tide,
To his appointed hour;
Yours to become all that we were,
And all we might have been;
Yours the fine eye that separates
The unseen from the seen.

[1] Written for the Centennial Celebration at Andover Phillips Academy.

THE UNSEEN COMRADES.[1]
Last night I saw an armèd band, whose feet
Did take the martial step, although they trod
Soundless as waves of light upon the air.
(Silent from silent lips the bugle fell.)
The wind was wild; but the great flag they bore,
Hung motionless, and glittered like a god
Above their awful faces while they marched.
And when I saw, I understood and said
"If these are they whom we did love, and give,
What seek they?" But one sternly answered me,
"We seek our comrades whom we left to thee:
The weak, who were thy strength; the poor, who had
Thy pride; the faint and few who gave to thee
One supreme hour from out the day of life,
One deed majestic to their century.
These were thy trust: how fare they at thy hands?
Thy saviors then, are they thy heroes now?
Our comrades still; we keep the step with them,
Behold! As thou unto the least of them
Shalt do, so dost thou unto us. Amen."

[1] Written for the benefit of the Soldiers' Home at Chelsea, Massachusetts.

STRONGER THAN DEATH

Who shall tell the story
As it was?
Write it with the heart's blood?
(Pale ink, alas!)
Speak it with the soul's lips,
Or be dumb?
Tell me, singers fled, and
Song to come!

No answer; like a shell the silence curls,
And far within it leans a whisper out,
Breathless and inarticulate, and whirls
And dies as dies an ailing dread or doubt.

And I, since there is found none else than I,
No stronger, sweeter voice than mine, to tell
This tale of love that cannot stoop to die
Were fain to be the whisper in the shell;

Were fain to lose and spend myself within
The sacred silence of one mighty heart,
And leaning from it, hidden there, to win
Some finer ear that, listening, bends apart.

"Fly for your lives!" The entrails of the earth
Trembled, resounding to the cry,
That, like a chasing ghost, around the mine
Crept ghastly: "The pit's on fire! Fly!"

The shaft, a poisoned throat whose breath was death,
Like hell itself grown sick of sin,
Hurled up the men; haggard and terrible;
Leaping upon us through the din

That all our voices made; and back we shrank
From them as from the starting dead;
Recoiling, shrieked, but knew not why we shrieked;
And cried, but knew not what we said.

And still that awful mouth did toss them up:
"The last is safe! The last is sound!"
We sobbed to see them where they sunk and crawled,
Like beaten hounds, upon the ground.

Some sat with lolling, idiot head, and laughed;
One reached to clutch the air away
His gasping lips refused; some cursed; and one
Knelt down, but he was old, to pray.

We huddled there together all that night,
Women and men from the wild Town;
I heard a shrill voice cry, "We all are up,
But some, ye have forgot, are down!"

"Who is forgot?" We stared from face to face;
But answering through the dark, she said
(It was a woman): "Eh, ye need not fret;
None is forgot except the dead.

"The buried dead asleep there in the works
Eh, Lord! It must be hot below!
Ye 'll keep 'em waking all the livelong night,
To set the mine a-burning so!"

And all the night the mine did burn and burst,
As if the earth were but a shell
Through which a child had thrust a finger-touch,
And, peal on dreadful peal, the bell,

The miner's 'larum, wrenched the quaking air;
And through the flaring light we saw
The solid forehead of the eternal hill
Take on a human look of awe;

As if it were a living thing, that spoke
And flung some protest to the sky,
As if it were a dying thing that saw,
But could not tell, a mystery.

The bells ran ringing by us all that night.
The bells ceased jangling with the morn.
About the blackened works, sunk, tossed, and rent,
We gathered in the foreign dawn;

Women and men, with eyes askance and strange,
Fearing, we knew not what, to see.
Against the hollowed jaws of the torn hill,
Why creep the miners silently?

From man to man, a whisper chills: "See, see,
The sunken shaft of Thirty-one!
The earth, a traitor to her trust, has fled
And turned the dead unto the sun.

"And here, O God of life and death! Thy work,
Thine only, this!" With foreheads bare,
We knelt, and drew him, young and beautiful,
Thirty years dead, into the air.

Thus had he perished; buried from the day;

By the swift poison caught and slain;
By the kind poison unmarred, rendered fair
Back to the upper earth again

The warm and breathing earth that knew him not;
And men and women wept to see
For kindred had he none among us all
How lonely even the dead may be.

We wept, I say; we wept who knew him not;
But sharp, a tearless woman sprang
From out the crowd (that quavering voice I knew),
And terrible her cry outrang:

"I pass, I pass ye all! Make way! Stand back!
Mine is the place ye yield," she said.
"He was my lover once, my own, my own;
Oh, he was mine, and he is dead!"

Women and men, we gave her royal way;
Proud as young joy the smile she had.
We knew her for a neighbor in the Town,
Unmated, solitary, sad.

Youth, hope, and love, we gave her silent way,
Calm as a sigh she swept us all;
Then swiftly, as a word leans to a thought,
We saw her lean to him, and fall

Upon the happy body of the dead
An aged woman, poor and gray.
Bright as the day, immortal as young Love,
And glorious as life, he lay.

Her shrunken hands caressed his rounded cheek,
Her white locks on his golden hair
Fell sadly. "O love!" she cried with shriveled lips,
"O love, my love, my own, my fair!

"See, I am old, and all my heart is gray.
They say the dead are aye forgot
There, there, my sweet! I whisper, leaning low,
That all these women hear it not.

"Deep in the darkness there, didst think on me?
High in the heavens, have ye been true?
Since I was young, and since you called me fair,
I never loved a man but you.

And here, my boy, you lie, so safe, so still"
But there she hushed; and in the dim,

Cool morning, timid as a bride, but calm
As a glad mother, gathered him

Unto her heart. And all the people then,
Women and men, and children too,
Crept back, and back, and back, and on,
Still as the morning shadows do.

And left them in the lifting dawn, they two,
On her sad breast, his shining head
Stirred softly, as were he the living one,
And she had been the moveless dead.

And yet we crept on, back, and back, and on.
The distance widened like the sky,
Between our little restlessness,
And Love so godlike that it could not die.

II.

VITTORIA.

Wise was the word the wise man spake, who said,
"Angelo was the only man to whom God gave
Four souls," the soul of sculpture and of song,
Of architecture and of art; these all.
For so God loved him, as if he were
His only child, and grouped about those brows
Ideals of Himself, not angels mild
As those that flit and beckon other lives,
But cherubim and seraphim; tall, strong,
Unsleeping, terrible; with wings across
Their mighty feet; and eyes, if we would look
Upon their blazing eyes, these too are hid
Some angels are all wings! Oh, shine and fly!
Were ye not angels, ye would strike us blind.

And yet they did not, could not dazzle her
That one sweet woman unto whom he bent
As pliant as the quarried marble turned
To life immortal in his own great hand.
Steadfast, Vittoria looked on Angelo.
She lifted lonely eyes. The years trod slow.
Fourfold the reverence which he gave to her,
Fourfold the awful tenderness, fourfold
The loyalty, the trust. And oh, fourfold
The comfort, beyond all power of comforting,
Whereby a lesser man may heal the hurt
Of widowhood!

Pescara had one soul
A little one; and it was stained. And he
It too, perhaps (God knows!) was dead.
The dead are God's.

Vittoria had one heart.
The woman gave it, and the woman gives
Once. Angelo was too late. And one who dared
To shed a tear for him, has dropped it here.

NEW NEIGHBORS.

Within the window's scant recess,
Behind a pink geranium flower,
She sits and sews, and sews and sits,
From patient hour to patient hour.

As woman-like as marble is,
Or as a lovely death might be
A marble death condemned to make
A feint at life perpetually.

Wondering, I watch to pity her;
Wandering, I go my restless ways;
Content, I think the untamed thoughts
Of free and solitary days,

Until the mournful dusk begins
To drop upon the quiet street,
Until, upon the pavement far,
There falls the sound of coming feet:

A happy, hastening, ardent sound,
Tender as kisses on the air
Quick, as if touched by unseen lips
Blushes the little statue there;

And woman-like as young life is,
And woman-like as joy may be,
Tender with color, lithe with love,
She starts, transfigured gloriously.

Superb in one transcendent glance
Her eyes, I see, are burning black
My little neighbor, smiling, turns,
And throws my unasked pity back.

I wonder, is it worth the while,
To sit and sew from hour to hour
To sit and sew with eyes of black,

Behind a pink geranium flower?

BY THE HEARTH.
You come too late;
'Tis far on in November.
The wind strikes bleak
Upon the cheek
That careth rather to keep warm,
(And where 's the harm?)
Than to abate
One jot of its calm color for your sake.
Watch! See! I stir the ember
Upon my lonely hearth and bid the fire wake.

And think you that it will?
'T is burned, I say, to ashes.
It smoulders cold
As grave-yard mould.
I wish indeed you would not blow
Upon it so!
The dead to kill.
I say, the ghosts of fires will never stir,
Nor woman lift the lashes
Of eyes wept dim, howe'er yours shine for love of her!

Ah, sweet surprise! did not think such shining
Upon the gloom
Of this cold room
Could fall. Your even, strong, calm breath
Calls life from death.
The warm light lies
At your triumphant feet, faint with desire
To reach you. See! The lining
Of violet and of silver in that sheath of fire!

If you would care
Although it is November
I will not say
A bitter nay
To such a gift for building fires.
And though it tires
Me to think of it, I'll own to you
(If you can stir the ember)
It may be found at last, just warm enough for two!

TOLD IN CONFIDENCE.
Vow you'll never, never tell him!

Freezing stars now glittering farthest, fairest on the winter sky;
If he woo me,
Not your coldest, cruel ray
Or can or may
Be found more chill and still to him than I.

Swear you'll never, never tell him!
Warm, red roses lifting your shy faces to the summer dew;
If he win me,
Blush your sweetest in his sight
For his delight,
But I can be as warm and sweet as you.

WHAT THE VIOLINS SAID.
SONG.

"We 're all for love," the violins said. SIDNEY LANIER.

Do I love you? Do I love you?
Ask the heavens that bend above you
To find language and to prove you
If they love the living sun.
Ask the burning, blinded meadows
If they love the falling shadows,
If they hold the happy shadows
When the fervid day is done.

Ask the blue-bells and the daisies,
Lost amid the hot field-mazes,
Lifting up their thirsty faces,
If they love the summer rains.
Ask the linnets and the plovers,
In the nest-life made for lovers,
Ask the bees and ask the clovers
Will they tell you for your pains?

Do I, Darling, do I love you?
What, I pray, can that behoove you?
How in Love's name can I move you?
When for Love's sake I am dumb!
If I told you, if I told you,
Would that keep you, would that hold you,
Here at last where I enfold you?
If it would - Hush! Darling, come!

WON.
Oh, when I would have loved you, Dear,

The sun of winter hung more near;
Yet not so sweet, so sweet, so sweet,
The wild-rose reddening at my feet.

Your lips had learned a golden word,
You sang a song that all men heard,
Oh, love is fleet, the strain is long.
Who stays the singer from her song?

Across my path the red leaves whirled.
Dared I to kneel with all the world?
How came I, then, to clasp you, Sweet,
And find a woman at my feet?

SPENT.

Heart of iron, smile of ice,
Oh! the rock.
See him stand as dumb as death.
If you could,
Would you care to stir or shock
Him, think you, by a blow or breath,
From his mood?

Arms of velvet, lips of love,
Oh! the wave.
See her creeping to his feet
Trustfully.
None shall know the sign he gave.
Death since then, were all too sweet.
Let her die.

Lift thine eyes upon the sea,
Soul of stone.
Rather (wouldst thou breathe or move?)
I would be
A warm wave, faithful, wasted, thrown,
Spent and rent and dead with love,
Than be thee.

PARTED.

Oh, never a word he answered,
And never a word spake she!
They turned their faces each from each,
And looked upon the sea.

The hands that cannot clasp for life,
Must quickly severed be.

The love that is not large enough
To live eternally,

In true love's name, for fair love's fame,
Must die before its bloom;
For it, in all God's earth or heaven,
There is no garden-room.

Though all the wine of life be lost,
Try well the red grape's hue.
Holy the soul that cannot taste
The false love for the true.

And blessed aye the fainting heart
For such a thirst shall be
Yet never a word they spoke, and looked
Upon the bitter sea.

AN APRIL GUST.
It shall be as it hath been.
All the world is glad and green
Hush! Ah, hush! There cannot be
April now for you and me.

Put your finger on the lips
Of your soul; the wild rain drips;
The wind goes diving down the sea;
Tell the wind, but tell not me.

Yet if I had aught to tell,
High as heaven, or deep as hell,
Bent the fates awry or fit,
I would find a word for it.

Oh, words that neither sea nor land
Can lift their ears to understand!
Wild words, as dumb as death or fear,
I dare to die, but not to hear!

THE ANSWER.
"That we together may sail,
Just as we used to do."
Carleton's Ballads.

And what if I should be kind?
And what if you should be true?
The old love could never go on,

Just as it used to do.

The wan, white hands of the waves
That smote us swift apart,
Will never enclasp again,
And draw us heart to heart.

The cold, far feet of the tides
That trod between us two,
Can never retrace their steps,
And fall where they used to do.

Oh, well the ships must remember,
That go down to the awful sea,
No keel that chisels the current
Can cut where it used to be.

Not a throb of the gloom or the glory
That stirs in the sun or the rain,
Will ever be that gloom or glory
That dazzled or darkened again.

Not a wave that stretches its arms,
And yearns to the breast of the shore,
Is ever the wave that came trusting,
And yearning, and loving, before.

The hope that is high as the heavens,
The joy that is keen as pain,
The faith that is free as the morning,
Can die, but can live not again.

And though I should step beside you,
And hand should reach unto hand,
We should walk mutely, stifled
Ghosts in a breathless land.

And what if I should be kind?
And though you should be true?
The old love could never, never
Love on as it used to do.

THORNS.
As we pass by the roses,
Into your finger-tip
Bruise you the thorn.
Quick at the prick you start,
Crying, "Alas, the smart!
Farewell, my pleasant friend,

Wisely our way we wend
Out of the reach of roses."

Oh, we pass by the roses!
Where does the red drop drip?
Where is the thorn?
What though 'tis hid and pressed
Piercing into my breast?
Scathless, I stretch my hand;
Strong as their roots I stand,
And dare to trust the roses.

THE INDIAN GIRL.
A PICTURE BY WALTER SHIRLAW.

She standeth silent as a thought
Too sacred to be uttered; all
Her face unfurling like a flower
That at a breath too near will shut.
Her life a little golden clock
Whose shining hands, arrested, stay
Forever at the hour of Love.

She doubts, she dares, she dreams, of what?
I ask; she, shrinking, answers not,
She swims before me, dim, a cup
Of waste, untasted tenderness.
I drink, I dread, until I seem
(Myself unto myself) to be
He whom she chose, and charmed, and missed,
On some faint Asiatic day
Of languorous summer, ages since.

SEALED.

"Shall I pour you the wine," she said,
"The wine that is rare and red?
Sweeter the cup for the drop."
"But why do you shrink and stop?"

"The seal of the wine
Has a sacred sign;
I am afraid," she said.

"I love and revere
You more for your fear,
Than I do for your wine," he said.

GUINEVERE.

Of Guinevere from Arthur separate,
And separate from Launcelot and the world,
And shielded in the convent with her sin,
As one draws fast a veil upon a face
That 's marred, but only holds the scar more close
Against the burning brain, I read to-day
This legend; and if other yet than I
Have read, or said, how know I? for the text
Was written in the story we have learned,
Between the ashen lines, invisible,
In hieroglyphs that blazed and leaped like light
Unto the eyes. A thousand times we read;
A thousand turn the page and understand,
And think we know the record of a life,
When lo! if we will open once again
The awful volume, hid, mysterious,
Intent, there lies the unseen alphabet
Re-reads the tale from breath to death, and spells
A living language that we never knew.

This that I read was one short song of hers,
A fragment, I interpret, or a lost
Faint prelude to another, missing too.
She sang it (says the text) one summer night,
After the vespers, when the Abbess passed
And blessed her; when the nuns were gone, and when
She, kneeling in her drowsy cell, had said
Her prayers (poor soul!), her sorrowful prayers, in which
She had besought the Lord, for His dear sake,
And love and pity of His Only Son,
To wash her of her stain, and make her fit
On summer nights, behind the convent bars
And on stone-floors, with bruisèd lips, to pray
Away all vision but repentance from her soul.

When, kneeling as she was, her limbs
Refused to bear her, and she fell afaint
From weariness and striving to become
A holy woman, all her splendid length
Upon the ground, and groveled there, aghast
That buried nature was not dead in her,
But lived, a rebel through her fair, fierce youth;
Aghast to find that clasped hands would clench;
Aghast to feel that praying lips refused
Like saints to murmur on, but shrank
And quivered dumb. "Alas! I cannot pray!"
Cried Guinevere. "I cannot pray! I will
Not lie! God is an honest God, and I
Will be an honest sinner to his face.

That rage of elemental tenderness,
The old, omnipotent caress she knows.
Yet once the solid earth did melt for her
And, pitying, made retreat before her flight;
Would she have hidden her forever there?
Or did she, wavering, linger long enough
To let the accustomed torrent chase her down?
Over the neck of the gorge,
I cling. Lean desperately!
He who feared a chasm's edge
Were never the one to see
The torment and the triumph hid
Where the deep surges be.
I pierce the gulf; I sweep the coast
Where wide the tide swings free;
I search as never soul sought before.
There is not patience enough in all the shore,
There is not passion enough in all the sea,
To tell my love for thee.

GALATEA.

A moment's grace, Pygmalion! Let me be
A breath's space longer on this hither hand
Of fate too sweet, too sad, too mad to meet.
Whether to be thy statue or thy bride
An instant spare me! Terrible the choice,
As no man knoweth, being only man;
Nor any, saving her who hath been stone
And loved her sculptor. Shall I dare exchange
Veins of the quarry for the throbbing pulse?
Insensate calm for a sure-aching heart?
Repose eternal for a woman's lot?
Forego God's quiet for the love of man?
To float on his uncertain tenderness,
A wave tossed up the shore of his desire,
To ebb and flow whene'er it pleaseth him;
Remembered at his leisure, and forgot,
Worshiped and worried, clasped and dropped at mood,
Or soothed or gashed at mercy of his will,
Now Paradise my portion, and now Hell;
And every single, several nerve that beats
In soul or body, like some rare vase, thrust
In fire at first, and then in frost, until
The fine, protesting fibre snaps?

Oh, who
Foreknowing, ever chose a fate like this?
What woman out of all the breathing world
Would be a woman, could her heart select,

Or love her lover, could her life prevent?
Then let me be that only, only one;
Thus let me make that sacrifice supreme,
No other ever made, or can, or shall.
Behold, the future shall stand still to ask,
What man was worth a price so isolate?
And rate thee at its value for all time.

For I am driven by an awful Law.
See! while I hesitate, it mouldeth me,
And carves me like a chisel at my heart.
'T is stronger than the woman or the man;
'T is greater than all torment or delight;
'T is mightier than the marble or the flesh.
Obedient be the sculptor and the stone!
Thine am I, thine at all the cost of all
The pangs that woman ever bore for man;
Thine I elect to be, denying them;
Thine I elect to be, defying them;
Thine, thine I dare to be, in scorn of them;
And being thine forever, bless I them!

Pygmalion! Take me from my pedestal,
And set me lower, lower, Love! that I
May be a woman, and look up to thee;
And looking, longing, loving, give and take
The human kisses worth the worst that thou
By thine own nature shalt inflict on me.

PART OF THE PRICE.

Take back, my friend, the gifts once given.
No fairer find I this side Heaven
With which to bless thee, than thine own
Resource of blessing. Mine alone
To render what is mine to lose.
No niggard am I with it. Choose!
Lavish, I keep not any part
Of that great price within my heart.
Wilt thou the quiet comfort have?
Thine be it, daily, to the grave!
The courage, shining down from one
Whose answering eyes put out the sun?
The tenderness that touched the nerve
Like music? Oh, I bid these serve
Thee, soothe thee, watchful of thy need
While mine is unattended; feed
Thy heart while mine goes famished. Glad,
I give the dearest thing I had.
Impoverished, can I find or spare

Aught else to thee of rich or rare?
Sweet thoughts that through the soul do sing,
And deeds like loving hands that cling,
And loyal faith, a sentry, nigh,
And prayers all rose-clouds hovering high?
Nay, nay; I keep not any. Hold
The wealth I leave with fingers cold
And trembling in thine own. One thing
Alone I do deny to bring
And give again to thee. Not now,
Nor ever, Dear, shalt thou learn how
To wrest it from me. Test thy strength!
By the world's measures, height or length
Too weak art thou, too weak to gain,
By sleight of tenderness or snatch of pain
At thine own most or least, to take from me
Mine own ideal lost, and saved, of thee.

EURYDICE.
Listening.

A PICTURE BY BURNE JONES.

I.
As sentient as a wedding-bell,
The vibrant air throbs calling her
Whose eager body, earwise curved,
Leans listening at the heart of hell.
She is one nerve of hearing, strained
To love and suffer, hope and fear
Thus, hearkening for her Love, she waits,
Whom no man's daring heart has gained.

II.
Oh, to be sound to such an ear!
Song, carol, vesper, comfort near,
Sweet words, at sweetest, whispered low,
Or dearer silence, happiest so.
By little languages of love
Her finer audience to prove;
A tenderness untried, to fit
To soul and sense so exquisite;
The blessed Orpheus to be
At last, to such Eurydice!

III.
I listened in hell! I listened in hell!
Down in the dark I heard your soul
Singing mine out to the holy sun.

Deep in the dark I heard your feet
Ringing the way of Love in hell.
Into the flame you strode and stood.
Out of the flame you bore me well,
As I listened in hell.

IV.
I listen in hell! I listen in hell!
Who trod the fire? Where was the scorch?
Clutched, clasped, and saved, what a tale was to tell
Heaven come down to hell!
Oh, like a spirit you strove for my sake!
Oh, like a man you looked back for your own!
Back, though you loved me heavenly well,
Back, though you lost me. The gods did decree,
And I listen in hell.

ELAINE AND ELAINE.
I.

Dead, she drifted to his feet.
Tell us, Love, is Death so sweet?

Oh! the river floweth deep.
Fathoms deeper is her sleep.

Oh! the current driveth strong.
Wilder tides drive souls along.

Drifting, though he loved her not,
To the heart of Launcelot,

Let her pass; it is her place.
Death hath given her this grace.

Let her pass; she resteth well.
What her dreams are, who can tell?

Mute the steersman; why, if he
Speaketh not a word, should we?

II.
Dead, she drifteth to his feet.
Close, her eyes keep secrets sweet.

Living, he had loved her well.
High as Heaven and deep as Hell.

Yet that voyage she stayeth not.

Wait you for her, Launcelot?

Oh! the river floweth fast.
Who is justified at last?

Locked her lips are. Hush! If she
Sayeth nothing, how should we?

III.

THE POET AND THE POEM.
Upon the city called the Friends'
The light of waking spring
Fell vivid as the shadow thrown
Far from the gleaming wing
Of a great golden bird, that fled
Before us loitering.

In hours before the spring, how light
The pulse of heaviest feet!
And quick the slowest hopes to stir
To measures fine and fleet.
And warm will grow the bitterest heart
To shelter fancies sweet.

Securely looks the city down
On her own fret and toil;
She hides a heart of perfect peace
Behind her veins' turmoil
A breathing-space removed apart
From out their stir and soil.

Our reverent feet that golden day
Stood in a quiet place,
That held repressed, I know not what
Of such a poignant grace
As falls, if dumb with life untold,
Upon a human face.

To fashion silence into words
The softest, teach me how!
I know the place is Silence caught
A-dreaming, then and now.
I only know 't was blue above,
And it was green below.

And where the deepening sunshine found
And held a holy mood,
Lowly and old, of outline quaint,

In mingled brick and wood,
Clasped in the arms of ivy vines
A nestling cottage stood:

A thing so hidden and so fair,
So pure that it would seem
Hewn out of nothing earthlier
Than a young poet's dream,
Of nothing sadder than the lights
That through the ivies gleam.

"Tell me," I said, while shrill the birds
Sang through the garden space,
To her who guided me, "tell me
The story of the place."
She lifted, in her Quaker cap,
A peaceful, puzzled face,

Surveyed me with an aged, calm,
And unpoetic eye;
And peacefully, but puzzled half,
Half tolerant, made reply:
"The people come to see that house
Indeed, I know not why,

"Except thee know the poem there
'T was written long since, yet
His name who wrote it, now, in fact
I cannot seem to get
His name who wrote that poetry
I always do forget.

"Hers was Evangeline; and here
In sound of Christ Church bells
She found her lover in this house,
Or so I've heard folks tell.
But most I know is, that's her name,
And his was Gabriel.

"I've heard she found him dying, in
The room behind that door,
(One of the Friends' old almshouses,
Perhaps thee 've heard before;)
Perhaps thee 've heard about her all
That I can tell, and more.

"Thee can believe she found him here,
If thee do so incline.
Folks have their fashions in belief
That may be one of thine.
I 'm sure his name was Gabriel,

And hers Evangeline."

She turned her to her common work
And unpoetic ways,
Nor knew the rare, sweet note she struck
Resounding to your praise,
O Poet of our common nights,
And of our care-worn days!

Translator of our golden mood,
And of our leaden hour!
Immortal thus shall poet gauge
The horizon of his power.
Wear in your crown of laurel leaves,
The little ivy flower!

And happy be the singer called
To such a lofty lot!
And ever blessed be the heart
Hid in the simple spot
Where Evangeline was loved and wept,
And Longfellow forgot.

O striving soul! strive quietly,
Whate'er thou art or dost,
Sweetest the strain, when in the song
The singer has been lost;
Truest the work, when 't is the deed,
Not doer, counts for most!

The shadow of the golden wing
Grew deep where'er it fell.
The heart it brooded over will
Remember long and well
Full many a subtle thing, too sweet
Or else too sad to tell.

Forever fall the light of spring
Fair as that day it fell,
Where Evangeline, led by your voice,
O solemn Christ Church bell!
For lovers of all springs, all climes,
At last found Gabriel.

OVERTASKED.
It was a weary hour,
I looked in the lily-bell.
How holy is the flower!
It leaned like an angel against the light;

"O soul!" it said, sighing, "be white, be white!"

I stretched my arms for rest,
I turned to the evening cloud
A vision how fair, how blest!
"Low heart," it called, softly, "arise and fly.
It were yours to reach levels as high as I."

I stooped to the hoary wave
That wept on the darkening shore.
It sobbed to me: "Oh, be brave!
Whatever you do, or dare, or will,
Like me to go striving, unresting still."

STRANDED.

O busy ships! that smile in sailing
In a glory
Like a dream,
From the colors of the harbor to the colors of the sea.
In singing words or in bewailing,
Tell the story
As you gleam,
Tell the story, guess the language of my idle hours for me.

O busy waves! so blest in bruising
Your white faces
On the shore.
So happy to be wasted with the purpose of the sea,
Content to leave with it the choosing
Of your places
Evermore,
Whisper but the far sea-meaning of my stranded life for me.

Gray the sails grow in departing
Like fleet swallows
To the South.
Stern the tide turns in its parting,
As it follows
With dumb mouth.
In the stillness and the sternness God makes answer unto me.

GLOUCESTER HARBOR.

One shadow glides from the dumb shore,
And one from every silent sail.
One cloud the averted heavens wear,
A soft mask, thin and frail.

Oh, silver is the lessening rain,
And yellow was the weary drouth.
The reef her warning finger puts
Upon the harbor's mouth.

Her thin, wan finger, stiff and stark,
She holds by night, she holds by day.
Ask, if you will. No answer makes
The sombre, guarded bay.

The fleet, with idle canvas hung,
Like a brute life, sleeps patiently.
The headlights nod across the cliff,
The fog blows out to sea.

There is no color on the tide,
No color on the helpless sky;
Across the beach, a safe, small sound
The grass-hid crickets cry.

And through the dusk I hear the keels
Of home-bound boats grate low and sweet.
O happy lights! O watching eyes!
Leap out the sound to greet.

O tender arms that meet and clasp!
Gather and cherish while ye may.
The morrow knoweth God. Ye know
Your own are yours to-day.

Forever from the Gloucester winds
The cries of hungry children start.
There breaks in every Gloucester wave
A widowed woman's heart.

THE TERRIBLE TEST.

Separate, upon the folded page
Of myth or marvel, sad or glad,
The test that gave the Lord to thee,
And thee to us, O Galahad!

"Found pure in deed, and word, and thought,"
The creature of our dream and guess,
The vision of the brain thou art,
The eidolon of holiness.

Man with the power of the God,
Man with the weaknesses of men,
Whose lips the Sangreal leaned to feed,

"Whose strength was the strength of ten,"

We read, and smile; no man thou wast;
No human pulses thine could be;
With downcast eyes we read, and sigh;
So terrible is purity!

O fairest legend of the years,
With folded wings, go, silently!
O flower of knighthood, yield your place
To One who comes from Galilee!

To wounded feet that shrink and bleed,
But press and climb the narrow way,
The same old way our own must step,
Forever, yesterday, to-day.

For soul can be what soul hath been,
And feet can tread where feet have trod.
Enough, to know that once the clay
Hath worn the features of the God.

MY DREAMS ARE OF THE SEA.

My dreams are of the Sea.
All night the living waters stepped
Stately and steadily. All night the wind
Conducted them. With forehead high, a rock,
Glittering with joy, stood to receive the shock
Of the flood-tide. I saw it in the mind
Of sleep and silence. When I woke, I wept.

My dreams are of the Sea.
But oh, it is the Sea of Glass!
I met that other tide as I desired.
Alone, the rock and I leaned to the wave,
A foolish suicide, that scooped its grave
Within the piteous sand. Now I am tired.
It died and it was buried. Let me pass.

SONG.

The firelight listens on the floor
To hear the wild winds blow.
Within, the bursting roses burn,
Without, there slides the snow.

Across the flower I see the flake
Pass mirrored, mystic, slow.

Oh, blooms and storms must blush and freeze,
While seasons come and go!

I lift the sash, and live, the gale
Comes leaping to my call.
The rose is but a painted one
That hangs upon the wall.

AN INTERPRETATION.
CHOPIN.
Prelude in C Minor, Opus 28.

From whirlwind to shower,
From noon-glare to shadow,
From the plough to the vesper,
A day is gone.
From passion to purpose,
From turmoil to rest,
From discord to harmony,
Life moveth on.

From terror and heartbreak,
From anger of anguish,
From vigil and famine,
A soul has gone.
By mercy of mystery,
Through trust which is best,
To feasting and sleeping now,
God calleth on.

THE SPHINX.[1]
O glad girls' faces, hushed and fair! how shall I sing for ye?
For the grave picture of a sphinx is all that I can see.

Vain is the driving of the sand, and vain the desert's art;
The years strive with her, but she holds the lion in her heart.

Baffled or fostered, patient still, the perfect purpose clings;
Flying or folded, strong as stone, she wears the eagle's wings.

Eastward she looks; against the sky the eternal morning lies;
Silent or pleading, veiled or free, she lifts the woman's eyes.

O grave girls' faces, listening kind! glad will I sing for ye,
While the proud figure of the sphinx is all that I can see.

[1] Written for a graduating class at Abbott Academy.

VICTURÆ SALUTAMUS.[1]

Shall we who are about to live,
Cry like a clarion on the battle-field?
Or weep before 't is fought, the fight to yield?
Thou that hast been and yet that art to be
Named by our name, that art the First and Last!
Womanhood of the future and the past!
Thee we salute, below the breath. Oh, give
To us the courage of our mystery.
Pealing, the clock of Time
Has struck the Woman's Hour....
We hear it on our knees. For ah, no power
Is ours to trip too lightly to the rhyme
Of idle words that fan the summer air,
Of bounding words that leap the years to come.
Ideal of ourselves! We dream and dare.
Victuræ salutamus! Thou art dumb.

[1] Written for the first commencement at Smith College.

THE ERMINE.

I read of the ermine to-day,
Of the ermine who will not step
By the feint of a step in the mire,
The creature who will not stain
Her garment of wild, white fire;

Of the dumb, flying, soulless thing
(So we with our souls dare to say),
The being of sense and of sod,
That will not, that will not defile
The nature she took from her God.

And we, with the souls that we have,
Go cheering the hunters on
To a prey with that pleading eye.
She cannot go into the mud!
She can stay like the snow, and die!

The hunters come leaping on.
She turns like a heart at bay.
They do with her as they will.
... O thou who thinkest on this!
Stand like a star, and be still,

Where the soil oozes under thy feet.

Better, ah, better to die
Than to take one step in the mire!
Oh, blessed to die or to live,
With garments of holy fire!

UNQUENCHED.[1]
I think upon the conquering Greek who ran
(Brave was the racer!) that brave race of old
Swifter than hope his feet that did not tire.

Calmer than love the hand which reached that goal;
A torch it bore, and cherished to the end,
And rescued from the winds the sacred fire.

O life the race! O heart the racer! Hush!
And listen long enough to learn of him
Who sleeps beneath the dust with his desire.

Go! shame thy coward weariness, and wail.
Who doubles contest, doubles victory.
Go! learn to run the race, and carry fire.

O Friend! The lip is brave, the heart is weak.
Stay near. The runner faints, the torch falls pale.
Save me the flame that mounteth ever higher!

Grows it so dark? I lift mine eyes to thine;
Blazing within them, steadfast, pure, and strong,
Against the wind there fights the eternal fire.

[1] At the Promethean and other festivals, young men ran with torches or lamps lighted from the sacrificial altar. "In this contest, only he was victorious whose lamp remained unextinguished in the race."

THE KING'S IMAGE.
Of iron were his arms; they could have held
The need of half the kingdom up; and in
His brow were iron atoms too. Thus was
He built. His heart, observe, was wrought of gold,
Burnished; it dazzled one to look at it.
His feet were carved of clay, and so he fell.

Clay unto clay shall perish and return.
The tooth of rust shall gnaw the iron down.
The conqueror of time, gold must endure.

Thou great amalgam! Suffering in thyself,

The while inflicting still the certain fate
Of thy disharmony. From Nature's law,
Unto her law, thy doom appeals; bids thee
To fear the metal sinews of thy soul,
And scorn the dust on which thou totterest;
But save, oh, save the heart of gold for one
Who did, beholding, trust in it.

IV.

AT THE PARTY.

Half a dozen children
At our house!
Half a dozen children
Quiet as a mouse,
Quiet as a moonbeam,
You could hear a pin
Waiting for the party
To begin.

Such a flood of flounces!
(Oh dear me!)
Such a surge of sashes
Like a silken sea.
Little eyes demurely
Cast upon the ground,
Little airs and graces
All around.

High time for that party
To begin!
To sit so any longer
Were a sort of sin;
As if you were n't acquainted
With society.
What a thing to tell of
That would be!

Up spoke a little lady
Aged five;
"I 've tumbled up my over-dress,
Sure as I 'm alive!
My dress came from Paris;
We sent to Worth for it;
Mother says she calls it
Such a fit!"

Quick there piped another
Little voice

"I did n't send for dresses,
Though I had my choice;
I have got a doll that
Came from Paris too;
It can walk and talk as
Well as you!"

Still, till now, there sat one
Little girl;
Simple as a snow-drop,
Without flounce or curl.
Modest as a primrose,
Soft, plain hair brushed back,
But the color of her dress was
Black, all black.

Swift she glanced around with
Sweet surprise;
Bright and grave the look that
Widened in her eyes.
To entertain the party
She must do her share,
As if God had sent her
Stood she there;

Stood a minute, thinking,
With crossed hands
How she best might meet the
Company's demands.
Grave and sweet the purpose
To the child's voice given:
"I have a little brother
Gone to Heaven!"

On the little party
Dropped a spell;
All the little flounces
Rustled where they fell;
But the modest maiden
In her mourning gown,
Unconscious as a flower,
Looketh down.

Quick my heart besought her,
Silently.
"Happy little maiden,
Give, O give to me
The highness of your courage,
The sweetness of your grace,
To speak a large word, in a
Little place."

A JEWISH LEGEND.

I like that old, kind legend
Not found in Holy Writ,
And wish that John or Matthew
Had made Bible out of it.

But though it is not Gospel,
There is no law to hold
The heart from growing better
That hears the story told:

How the little Jewish children
Upon a summer day,
Went down across the meadows
With the Child Christ to play.

And in the gold-green valley,
Where low the reed-grass lay,
They made them mock mud-sparrows
Out of the meadow clay.

So, when these all were fashioned,
And ranged in rows about,
"Now," said the little Jesus,
"We'll let the birds fly out."

Then all the happy children
Did call, and coax, and cry
Each to his own mud-sparrow:
"Fly, as I bid you! Fly!"

But earthen were the sparrows,
And earth they did remain,
Though loud the Jewish children
Cried out, and cried again.

Except the one bird only
The little Lord Christ made;
The earth that owned Him Master,
His earth heard and obeyed.

Softly He leaned and whispered:
"Fly up to Heaven! Fly!"
And swift, His little sparrow
Went soaring to the sky,

And silent, all the children
Stood, awestruck, looking on,

Till, deep into the heavens,
The bird of earth had gone.

I like to think, for playmate
We have the Lord Christ still,
And that still above our weakness
He works His mighty will,

That all our little playthings
Of earthen hopes and joys
Shall be, by His commandment,
Changed into heavenly toys.

Our souls are like the sparrows
Imprisoned in the clay,
Bless Him who came to give them wings
Upon a Christmas Day!

V.

THE SONGS OF SEVENTY YEARS.
J. G. W.

Master! let stronger lips than these
Turn melody to harmony,
Poet! mine tremble as they crave
A word alone with thee.

Thy songs melt on the vibrant air,
The wild birds know them, and the wind;
The common light hath claim on them,
The common heart and mind.

And air, and light, and wind, shall be
Thy fellow-singers, while they say
How seventy years of music stir
The common pulse to-day.

Hush, sweetest songs! Mine ears are deaf
To all of ye save only one.
Blind are the eyes that turn the leaf
Against the Autumn sun.

Oh, blinder once were fading eyes,
Close folded now from shine and rain,
And duller were the dying ears
That heard the chosen strain.

Stay, solemn chant! 'T is mine to sing

Your notes alone below the breath.
'T is mine to bless the poet who
Can bless the hour of death.

For once a spirit "sighed for home,"
A "longed-for light whereby to see,"
And "wearied," found the way to them,
O Christian seer, through thee!

Passed, with thy words on paling lips,
Passed, with thy courage to depart;
Passed, with thy trust within the soul,
Thy music in the heart.

Oh, calm above our restlessness,
And rich beyond our dreaming, yet
In heaven, I know, one owes to thee
A glad and grateful debt.

From it may learn some tenderer art,
May find and take some better way
Than all our tenderest and best,
To crown thy life to-day.

BIRTHDAY VERSES.

H. B. S.

Arise, and call her blessed, seventy years!
Each one a tongue to speak for her, who needs
No poor device of ours to tell to-day
The story of her glory in our hearts.
Precede us all, ye quiet lips of love,
Ye honors high of home, nobilities
Of mother and of wife, the heraldry
Of happiness; dearer to her than were
The homage of the world. We yield unto
The royal claims of tenderness. Speak thou
Before all voices, ripened human life!

Arise, and call her blessed, dark-browed men!
She put the silver lyre aside for you.
She could not stroll across the idle strings
Of fancy, while you wept uncomforted,
But rang upon the fetters of a race
Enchained, the awful chord which pealed along,
And echoed in the cannon-shot that broke
The manacle, and bade the bound go free.
She brought a Nation on its knees for shame,
She brought a world into a black slave's heart.
Where are our lighter laurels? O my friends!

Brothers and sisters of the busy pen,
Five million freemen crown her birthday feast,
Before whose feet our little leaf we lay.

Arise and call her blessed, fainting souls!
For whom she sang the strains of holy hope.
Within the gentle twilight of her days,
Like angels, bid her own hymns visit her.
Her life no ivy-tangled door, but wide
And welcome to His solemn feet, who need
Not knock for entrance, nor one ever ask
"Who cometh there?" so still and sure the step,
So well we know God doth "abide in her."

Oh, wait to make her blessed, happy world!
To which she looketh onward, ardently.
Lie in fair distance far, ye streets of gold,
Where up and down light-hearted spirits walk,
And wonder that they stayed so long away.
Be patient for her coming, for our sakes,
Who will love Heaven better, keeping her.
This only ask we: When from prayer to praise
She moves, and when from peace to joy; be hers
To know she hath the life eternal, since
Her own heart's dearest wish did meet her there.

A TRIBUTE.

Blinded I groped, you gave me sight.
Perplexed I turned, you sent me light.
You speak unto a thousand ears:
I pay you tribute in hid tears.
I pay you homage in the hopes
That rise to scale life's scathèd slopes.
I give you gratitude in this:
That, midway on the precipice
You never trod and never saw,
Where air you never drank, strikes raw
And wan upon the wasted breath,
And gulfs you never passed, gape death,
And crags you gained some sunlit way
Frown threatening over me to-day,
That here with bruisèd hand I cling,
Because I heard you yonder sing
With those who conquer. If through joy,
Then deeper be our shame who toy
And loiter in the scourging rain,
And did not pass by strength of pain.
Laggard below, I reach to bless
You who are King of happiness;

You are the victor, you the brave,
Who could not stoop to be her slave.
Downward to me, rebuking, fling
My privilege of suffering.
I take and listen. Teach me. See!
Nearer than you, I ought to be;
Nearer the height man never trod,
Nearer the veiled face of God.
I ought, and am not. Comrade! be
Unconscious captain unto me.
Unknowing, beckon and command:
I answer you with unseen hand.
You read in vain these lines between,
And smiling, wonder whom I mean.

TO O. W. H.
AUGUST 29, 1879.
I had no song so wise and sweet,
As birthday songs, dear friend, should be.
Silent, among a hundred guests,
I only prayed for thee.

Such wishes held the speaking lip,
Such mood of blessing took me, there,
That music, like a bird to heaven,
Flew, and was lost in prayer.

WHOSE SHALL THE WELCOME BE?
H. W. L.
The wave goes down, the wind goes down,
The gray tide glitters on the sea,
The moon seems praying in the sky.
Gates of the New Jerusalem
(A perfect pearl each gate of them)
Wide as all heaven swing on high;
Whose shall the welcome be?

The wave went down, the wind went down,
The tide of life turned out to sea;
Patience of pain and grace of deed,
The glories of the heart and brain,
Treasure that shall not come again;
The human singing that we need,
Set to a heavenly key.

The wave goes down, the wind goes down,
All tides at last turn to the sea.

We learn to take the thing we have.
Thou who hast taught us strength in grief,
As moon to shadow, high and chief,
Shine out, white soul, beyond the grave,
And light our loss of thee!

EXEAT.

To the hope that he has taught,
To the beauty he has wrought,
To the comfort he has been;
To the dream that poets tell,
To the land where Gabriel
Can not lose Evangeline;
Hush! let him go.

GEORGE ELIOT.[1]

At evening once, the lowly men who loved
Our Master were found desolate, and grieved
For Him whose eyes had been the glory of
Their lives. He, silent, followed them, and joined
Himself unto their sorrow; with the voice
Of love that liveth past the end, and yearns
Like empty arms across the sepulchre,
Did comfort them. They heard, and knew Him not.

At eventide, O Lord, one trod for us
The solitary way of a great Soul;
Whereof the peril, pain, and debt, alone
He knows, who marked the road.
We watched, and held
Her in our arms of prayer. We wept, and said:
Our sister hath a heavy hurt. We bow,
And cry: The crown is buried with the Queen.

At twilight, as she, groping, sought for rest,
What solemn footfall echoed down the dark?
What tenderness that would not let her go?
And patience that Love only knoweth, paced
Silent, beside her, to the last, faint step?
What scarred Hand gently caught her as she sank?
Thou being with her, though she knew Thee not.

[1] The last book which she read was Thomas à Kempis's Imitation of Christ.

HER JURY.

A lily rooted in a sacred soil,
Arrayed with those who neither spin nor toil;
Dinah, the preacher, through the purple air,
Forever in her gentle evening prayer
Shall plead for Her, what ear too deaf to hear?
"As if she spoke to some one very near."

And he of storied Florence, whose great heart
Broke for its human error; wrapped apart,
And scorching in the swift, prophetic flame
Of passion for late holiness; and shame
Than untried glory grander, gladder, higher
Deathless, for Her, he "testifies by fire."

A statue fair and firm on shining feet,
Womanhood's woman, Dorothea, sweet
As strength, and strong as tenderness, to make
A "struggle with the dark" for white light's sake,
Immortal stands, unanswered speaks. Shall they,
Of Her great hand the moulded, breathing clay,
Her fit, select, and proud survivors be?
Possess the life eternal, and not She?

VI.

A PRAYER.
MATINS.

Lord, Thou hast promised. Lo! I give Thee back
Thine own great Word. Keep it. I summon Thee.
Keep it as God can, not as men do. See,
Great God! who art to us the awful Truth
Whereby we live, and move, and know the true
I ask Thee to be true unto Thyself.

There is a soul that has not sinned unto
The death. I pray for it. To such as seek
For such a one, O Power invisible!
O Mystery and Mercy! Thou hast said
Thou hearkenest. I dare remind Thee, God.

I dare appeal unto Thine honor. Hear!
Fulfill Thy pledge to me.
God, God! Great God!
I pour my soul out, dash it down awaste
Like water, as I would my life, to save
This other one. I light my words with fire,
Like fagots scorching all my shrinking heart.
So would I walk in fire with these my feet
Of flesh, if that could melt this frozen heart

I pray for.
Thou who listenest! Dumb God!
Had I Thy dreadful power to turn the souls
Of men as they were rivers in Thy hand,
Then would I have this noble one. I would
Not lose its loyalty. I tell Thee, Lord,
If I had made it, then it sure should love
And honor me.
Hearken to me! Oh, save!
Give me mine answer! Save!
Great God,
I summon Thee! I summon Thee!

Father,
I am Thy child. If I have asked too much,
Or asked or longed amiss in any wise,
Or read awry Thy Word mysterious,
Or made one cry unworthy of a child,
I pray Thee to deny me all I ask
Unto my asking, and rebuke me so.
And if Thou savest, Lord, dear Lord, dear Lord!
Then let it be because some worthier
Than I, did pray.....

AN ACKNOWLEDGMENT.
For the faith that is not broken

By the burden of the day;
For the word that is not spoken
(Dearest words are slow to say);
For the golden draught unproffered
To the thirst that thirsteth on;
For the hand that is not offered
When the struggling strength is gone;
For the sturdy heart that will not
Make a pauper of my need;
Friend, I mean sometime to thank thee,
From my soul, in truth and deed.
Wait! Some day, when I am braver,
I will do so, say so. Now
(Oh! be tender!) I am tired;
I have forgotten how.

HYMN.
FOR A BROTHER'S INSTALLATION.
Lord, are there any stones upon the way,
That tear Thy bleeding feet?

If our weak hands can move them from Thy path,
Give us that duty sweet.

Is there, O patient and pathetic Face!
One thorn upon Thy brow
That we can pluck from out Thy cruel crown?
For we would do it now.

Is there a deed so difficult for us
That none but Thou canst ask?
Thine asking be our answering. Lo! swift
Be ours that happy task.

Lord, hast Thou left Thy hungry in the world
For us to find, to feed?
Sharper the hungers of the soul. Give us
Nutrition for that need.

And hast Thou prisoners unvisited,
Whose woes our care should tell?
There is a deeper prison of the heart;
Help us to find that cell.

Is there a mourner dear to Thee, whom we
Have left uncomforted?
Yet still through lonelier loneliness, the heart
Bereft of Thee, is led.

O world of common, human cries! and calls
Of souls in direst need!
To meet ye, mighty were the love that sought
To take the Master's speed.

Give us that love, dear God, who gave to us
To bear His loving name.
Give us that sacred speed to keep the step
That strikes with His the same.

Waves of one tide, this people be! and flow
Straight shoreward to Thy will.
White as a dove, upon them, now descend
Thy Spirit, strong and still.

Thy blessings on their future rest and brood,
The brightest, lip can tell,
In home and heart, in faith and fact, O best
Of daily mercy! dwell.

With those who summon, trusting it to lead
Their feet to walk Christ's way
The voice of him on whose bowed head, I call

The grace of God to-day.

ANSWERED.

Why did I never sing a song to you?
Dearest! To you again, behold the question start.
To mine own pulses have I ever sung? Or do
I read a rhyme unto my beating heart?

WESTWARD.

My thoughts like waves creep up, creep on,
How patient is the sea!
How shall we climb, the tide and I
Up to the hills and thee?

Were waters free as winds, to go
Where mood or need might be,
They could but find the sky, above
The cañon as the sea.

THREE FRIENDS.

Oh, not to you, my mentor sweet,
And stern as only sweetness can,
Whose grave eyes look out steadfastly
Across my nature's plan,

And take unerring measure down
Where'er that plan is failed or foiled,
Thinking far less of purpose kept
Than of a vision spoiled.

And tender less to what I am,
Than sad for what I might have been;
And walking softly before God
For my soul's sake, I ween.

'T is not to you, my spirit leans,
O grave, true judge! When spent with strife,
And groping out of gloom for light,
And out of death for life.

Nor yet to you, who calmly weigh
And measure every grace and fault,
Whose martial nature never turns
From right to left, to halt

For any glamour of the heart,
Or any glow that ever is,
Grander than Truth's high noonday glare,
In love's sweet sunrises;

Who know me by the duller hues
Of common nights and common days,
And in their sober atmospheres
Find level blame and praise.

True hearts and dear! 't is not in you,
This fainting, warring soul of mine
Finds silver carven chalices,
To hold life's choicest wine

Unto its thirsty lips, and bid
It drink, and breathe, and battle on,
Till all its dreams are deeds at last,
And all its heights are won.

I turn to you, confiding love.
O lifted eyes! look trustfully,
Till Heaven shall lend you other light,
Like kneeling saints, on me.

And let me be to you, dear eyes,
The thing I am not, till I, too,
Shall see as I am seen, and stand
At last revealed to you.

And let me nobler than I am,
And braver still, eternally,
And finer, truer, purer, than
My finest, purest, be

To your sweet vision. There I stand
Transfigured fair in love's deceit,
And while your soul looks up to mine,
My heart lies at your feet.

Believe me better than my best,
And stronger than my strength can hold,
Until your magic faith transmute
My pebbles into gold.

I'll be the thing you hold me, Dear!
After I 'm dead, if not before
Nor, through the climbing ages, will
I give the conflict o'er.

But if upon the Perfect Peace,

And past the thing that was, and is,
And past the lure of voices, in
A world of silences,

A pain can crawl, a little one
A cloud upon a sunlit land;
I think in Heaven my heart must ache
That you should understand.

A NEW FRIEND.

The sun is sinking on the sacred lands
Wherein the grain ungarnered beckoning stands.

Who loses never finds, nor can, nor may,
The common, human glory of the day.

Close, let us enter, tear-blind as we must;
Reapers, not gleaners of a solemn trust.

AN ETCHING.

A true knight! Knowing neither worldly fear,
Nor yet reproach of her unworldly faith;
Fine eyes shall see, yet see not, on this page,
A man, who from a woman's heart of hearts
Could earn, and keep, the sacred name of Friend.

TO MY FATHER.

Tired with the little follies of the day,
A child crept, sobbing, to your arms to say
Her evening prayer; and if by God or you
Forgiven and loved, she never asked or knew.

With life's mistake and care too early old,
And spent with sorrow upon sorrow told,
She finds the father's heart the surest rest;
The earliest love shall be the last and best.

THE GATES BETWEEN.

Pearl-white, opaque and fixed fast,
Flashing between the hands unclasped,
Blinding between despairing eyes,
The awful Gates shut to, at last,

On comfort snatched, and anguish done,
On every moan beneath the sun,
Till we and ours, and joy are one.

This is your hour, Gates of God,
Your solemn hour, bars of gold,
But there shall come another yet.
Like silken sails you shall be furled,
Like melting mist you shall be set.

Oh, ye the dearest! vanished from
Love's little inner, sheltered spot.
To ye I whisper; not forgot,
But loved the dearer, namèd not.
Across the barrier old as life,
Lean to us from the Silent World.

A PRAYER.
VESPERS.
Great God!
Behold, I lie
Beneath Thine awful eye,
As the sea beneath the sky.

My God,
What hope abides?
Thine unknown purpose rides
The torrent of my tides.

Dear God,
I am not a shore, or hill,
An ocean must take still
The colors of the heavens' will.

Choose, God.
Though days be blue, or gold,
Though sorrows new, or cold,
Though purple joy be there,
Or gray of old despair,
Give but Thyself to me,
And let me be Thy sea.
Thy storms have had their way.
I pray now not to pray.

COMRADES

In the late May evening the soul of summer had gone suddenly incarnate, but the old man, indifferent and petulant, thrashed upon his bed. He was not used to being ill, and found no consolations in weather. Flowers regarded him observantly, one might have said critically, from the tables, the bureau, the window-sills: tulips, fleurs-de-lis, pansies, peonies, and late lilacs, for he had a garden-loving wife who made the most of "the dull season," after crocuses and daffodils, and before roses. But he manifested no interest in flowers; less than usual, it must be owned, in Patience, his wife. This was a marked incident. They had lived together fifty years, and she had acquired her share of the lessons of marriage, but not that ruder one given chiefly to women to learn, she had never found herself a negligible quantity in her husband's life. She had the profound maternal instinct which is so large an element in the love of every experienced and tender wife; and when Reuben thrashed profanely upon his pillows, staring out of the window above the vase of jonquils, without looking at her, clearly without thinking of her, she swallowed her surprise as if it had been a blue-pill, and tolerantly thought:

"Poor boy! To be a veteran and can't go!"

Her poor boy, being one-and-eighty, and having always had health and her, took his disappointment like a boy. He felt more outraged that he could not march with the other boys to decorate the graves to-morrow than he had been, or had felt that he was, by some of the important troubles of his long and, on the whole, comfortable life. He took it unreasonably; she could not deny that. But she went on saying "Poor boy!" as she usually did when he was unreasonable. When he stopped thrashing and swore no more she smiled at him brilliantly. He had not said anything worse than damn! But he was a good Baptist, and the lapse was memorable.

"Peter?" he said. "Just h'ist the curtain a mite, won't you? I want to see across over to the shop. Has young Jabez locked up everything? Somebody's got to make sure."

Behind the carpenter's shop the lush tobacco-fields of the Connecticut valley were springing healthily. "There ain't as good a crop as there gener'lly is," the old man fretted.

"Don't you think so?" replied Patience. "Everybody say it's better. But you ought to know."

In the youth and vigor of her no woman was ever more misnamed. Patient she was not, nor gentle, nor adaptable to the teeth in the saw of life. Like wincing wood, her nature had resented it, the whole biting thing. All her gentleness was acquired, and acquired hard. She had fought like a man to endure like a woman, to accept, not to writhe and rebel. She had not learned easily how to count herself out. Something in the sentimentality or even the piety of her name had always seemed to her ridiculous; they both used to have their fun at its expense; for some years he called her Impatience, degenerating into Imp if he felt like it. When Reuben took to calling her Peter, she found it rather a relief.

"You'll have to go without me," he said, crossly.

"I'd rather stay with you," she urged. "I'm not a veteran."

"Who'd decorate Tommy, then?" demanded the old man. "You wouldn't give Tommy the go-by, would you?"

"I never did, did I?" returned the wife, slowly.

"I don't know's you did," replied Reuben Oak, after some difficult reflection.

Patience did not talk about Tommy. But she had lived Tommy, so she felt, all her married life, ever since she took him, the year-old baby of a year-dead first wife who had made Reuben artistically miserable; not that Patience thought in this adjective; it was one foreign to her vocabulary; she was accustomed to say of that other woman: "It was better for Reuben. I'm not sorry she died." She added, "Lord forgive me," because she was a good church member, and felt that she must. Oh, she had "lived Tommy," God knew. Her own baby had died, and there were never any more. But Tommy lived and clamored at her heart. She began by trying to be a good stepmother. In the end she did not have to try. Tommy never knew the difference; and his father had long since forgotten it. She had made him so happy that he seldom remembered anything unpleasant. He was accustomed to refer to his two conjugal partners as "My wife and the other woman."

But Tommy had the blood of a fighting father, and when the Maine went down, and his chance came, he, too, took it. Tommy lay dead and nameless in the trenches at San Juan. But his father had put up a tall, gray slate-stone slab for him in the churchyard at home. This was close to the baby's; the baby's was little and white. So the veteran was used to "decorating Tommy" on Memorial Day. He did not trouble himself about the little, white gravestone then. He had a veteran's savage jealousy of the day that was sacred to the splendid heroisms and sacrifices of the sixties.

"What do they want to go decorating all their relations for?" he argued. "Ain't there three hundred and sixty-four days in the year for them?"

He was militant on this point, and Patience did not contend. Sometimes she took the baby's flowers over the day after.

"If you can spare me just as well's not, I'll decorate Tommy to-morrow," she suggested, gently. "We'll see how you feel along by that."

"Tommy's got to be decorated if I'm dead or livin'," retorted the veteran. The soldier father struggled up from his pillow, as if he would carry arms for his soldier son. Then he fell back weakly. "I wisht I had my old dog here," he complained -"my dog Tramp. I never did like a dog like that dog. But Tramp's dead, too. I don't believe them boys are coming. They've forgotten me, Peter. You haven't," he added, after some slow thought. "I don't know's you ever did, come to think."

Patience, in her blue shepherd-plaid gingham dress and white apron, was standing by the window, a handsome woman, a dozen years younger than her husband; her strong face was gentler than most strong faces are, in women; peace and pain, power and subjection, were fused upon her aspect like warring elements reconciled by a mystery. Her hair was not yet entirely white, and her lips were warm and rich. She had a round figure, not overgrown. There were times when she did not look over thirty. Two or three late jonquils that had outlived their calendar in a cold spot by a wall stood on the window-sill beside her; these trembled in the slant, May afternoon light. She stroked them in their vase, as if they had been frightened or hurt. She did not immediately answer Reuben, and, when she did, it was to say, abruptly:

"Here's the boys! They're coming, the whole of them! Jabez Trent, and old Mr. Succor, and David Swing on his crutches. I'll go right out 'n' let them all in."

She spoke as if they had been a phalanx. Reuben panted upon his pillows. Patience had shut the door, and it seemed to him as if it would never open. He pulled at his gray flannel dressing-gown with nervous fingers; they were carpenter's fingers, worn, but supple and intelligent. He had on his old red nightcap, and he felt the indignity, but he did not dare to take the cap off; there was too much pain underneath it.

When Patience opened the door she nodded at him girlishly. She had preceded the visitors, who followed her without speaking. She looked forty years younger than they did. She marshaled them as if she had been their colonel. The woman herself had a certain military look.

The veterans filed in slowly, three aged, disabled men. One was lame, and one was palsied; one was blind, and all were deaf.

"Here they are, Reuben," said Patience Oak. "They've all come to see you. Here's the whole Post."

Reuben's hand went to his red night-cap. He saluted gravely.

The veterans came in with dignity, David Swing, and Jabez Trent, and old Mr. Succor. David was the one on crutches, but Jabez Trent, with nodding head and swaying hand, led old Mr. Succor, who could not see.

Reuben watched them with a species of grim triumph. "I ain't blind," he thought, "and I hain't got the shakin' palsy. Nor I hain't come on crutches, either."

He welcomed his visitors with a distinctly patronizing air. He was conscious of pitying them as much as a soldier can afford to pity anything. They seemed to him very old men.

"Give 'em chairs, Peter," he commanded. "Give 'em easy chairs. Where's the cushions?"

"I favor a hard cheer myself," replied the blind soldier, sitting solid and straight upon the stiff bamboo chair into which he had been set down by Jabez Trent. "I'm sorry to find you so low, Reuben Oak."

"Low!" exploded the old soldier. "Why, nothing partikler ails me. I hain't got a thing the matter with me but a spell of rheumatics. I'll be spry as a kitten catchin' grasshoppers in a week. I can't march to-morrow, that's all. It's darned hard luck. How's your eyesight, Mr. Succor?"

"Some consider'ble better, sir," retorted the blind man. "I calc'late to get it back. My son's goin' to take me to a city eye-doctor. I ain't only seventy-eight. I'm too young to be blind. 'Tain't as if I was onto crutches, or I was down sick abed. How old are you, Reuben?"

"Only eighty-one!" snapped Reuben.

"He's eighty-one last March," interpolated his wife.

"He's come to a time of life when folks do take to their beds," returned David Swing. "Mebbe you could manage with crutches, Reuben, in a few weeks. I've been on 'em three years, since I was seventy-five. I've got to feel as if they was relations. Folks want me to ride to-morrow," he added, contemptuously, "but I'll march on them crutches to decorate them graves, or I won't march at all."

Now Jabez Trent was the youngest of the veterans; he was indeed but sixty-eight. He refrained from mentioning this fact. He felt that it was indelicate to boast of it. His jerking hand moved over toward the bed, and he laid it on Reuben's with a fine gesture.

"You'll be round, you'll be round before you know it," he shouted.

"I ain't deef," interrupted Reuben, "like the rest of you." But the palsied man, hearing not at all, shouted on:

"You always had grit, Reuben, more'n most of as. You stood more, you was under fire more, you never was afraid of anything. What's rheumatics? 'Tain't Antietam."

"Nor it ain't Bull Run," rejoined Reuben. He lifted his red nightcap from his head. "Let it ache!" he said. "It ain't Gettysburg."

"It seems to me," suggested Jabez Trent, "that Reuben he's under fire just about now. He ain't used to bein' disabled. It appears to me he's fightin' this matter the way a soldier 'd oughter. Comrades, I move he's entitled to promotion for military conduct. He'd rather than sympathy, wouldn't you, Reuben?"

"I don't feel to deserve it," muttered Reuben. "I swore to-day. Ask my wife."

"No, he didn't!" blazed Patience Oak. "He never said a thing but damn. He's getting tired, though," she added, under breath. "He ain't very well." She delicately brushed the foot of Jabez Trent with the toe of her slipper.

"I guess we'd better not set any longer," observed Jabez Trent. The three veterans rose like one soldier. Reuben felt that their visit had not been what he expected. But he could not deny that he was tired out; he wondered why. He beckoned to Jabez Trent, who, shaking and coughing, bent over him.

"You'll see the boys don't forget to decorate Tommy, won't you?" he asked, eagerly. Jabez could not hear much of this, but he got the word Tommy, and nodded.

The three old men saluted silently, and when Reuben had put on his nightcap he found that they had all gone. Only Patience was in the room, standing by the jonquils, in her blue gingham dress and white apron.

"Tired?" she asked, comfortably. "I've mixed you up an egg-nog. Think you could take it?"

"They didn't stay long," complained the old man. "It don't seem to amount to much, does it?"

"You've punched your pillows all to pudding-stones," observed Patience Oak. "Let me fix 'em a little."

"I won't be fussed over!" cried Reuben, angrily. He gave one of his pillows a pettish push, and it went half across the room. Patience picked it up without remark. Reuben Oak held out a contrite hand.

"Peter, come here!" he commanded. Patience, with her maternal smile, obeyed.

"You stay, Peter, anyhow. Folks don't amount to anything. It's you, Peter."

Patience's eyes filled. But she hid them on the pillow beside him, he did not know why. She put up one hand and stroked his cheek.

"Just as if I was a johnnyquil," said the old man. He laughed, and grew quiet, and slept. But Patience did not move. She was afraid of waking him. She sat crouched and crooked on the edge of the bed, uncomfortable and happy.

Out on the street, between the house and the carpenter's shop, the figures of the veterans bent against the perspective of young tobacco. They walked feebly. Old Mr. Succor shook his head:

"Looks like he'd never see another Decoration Day. He's some considerable sick, an' he ain't young."

"He's got grit, though," urged Jabez Trent.

"He's pretty old," sighed David Swing. "He's consider'ble older'n we be. He'd ought to be prepared for his summons any time at his age."

"We'll be decorating him, I guess, come next year," insisted old Mr. Succor. Jabez Trent opened his mouth to say something, but he coughed too hard to speak.

"I'd like to look at Reuben's crop as we go by," remarked the blind man. "He's lucky to have the shop 'n' the crop too."

The three turned aside to the field, where old Mr. Succor appraised the immature tobacco leaves with seeing fingers.

"Connecticut's a great State!" he cried.

"And this here's a great town," echoed David Swing. "Look at the quota we sent, nigh a full company. And we had a great colonel," he added, proudly. "I calc'late he'd been major-general if it hadn't 'a' been for that infernal shell."

"Boys," said Jabez Trent, slowly, "Memorial Day's a great day. It's up to us to keep it that way. Boys, we're all that's left of the Charles Darlington Post."

"That's a fact," observed the blind soldier, soberly.

"That's so," said the lame one, softly.

The three did not talk any more; they walked past the tobacco-field thoughtfully. Many persons carrying flowers passed or met them. These recognized the veterans with marked respect, and with some perplexity. What! Only old blind Mr. Succor? Just David Swing on his crutches, and Jabez Trent with the shaking palsy? Only those poor, familiar persons whom one saw every day, and did not think much about on any other day? Unregarded, unimportant, aging neighbors? These who had ceased to be useful, ceased to be interesting, who were not any longer of value to the town, or to the State, to their friends (if they had any left), or to themselves? Heroes? These plain, obscure old men? Heroes?

So it befell that Patience Oak "decorated Tommy" for his father that Memorial Day. The year was 1909. The incident of which we have to tell occurred twelve months thereafter, in 1910. These, as I have gathered them, are the facts:

Time, to the old, takes an unnatural pace, and Reuben Oak felt that the year had sprinted him down the race-track of life; he was inclined to resent his eighty-second March birthday as a personal insult;

but April cried over him, and May laughed at him, and he had acquired a certain grim reconciliation with the laws of fate by the time that the nation was summoned to remember its dead defenders upon their latest anniversary. This resignation was the easier because he found himself unexpectedly called upon to fill an extraordinary part in the drama and the pathos of the day.

He slept brokenly the night before, and waked early; it was scarcely five o'clock. But Patience, his wife, was already awake, lying quietly upon her pillow, with straight, still arms stretched down beside him. She was careful not to disturb him, she always was; she was so used to effacing herself for his sake that he had ceased to notice whether she did or not; he took her beautiful dedication to him as a matter of course; most husbands would, if they had its counterpart. In point of fact, and in saying this we express her altogether. Patience had the genius of love. Charming women, noble women, unselfish women may spend their lives in a man's company, making a tolerable success of marriage, yet lack this supreme gift of Heaven to womanhood, and never know it. Our defects we may recognize; our deficiencies we seldom do, and the love deficiency is the most hopeless of human limitations. Patience was endowed with love as a great poet is by song, or a musician by harmony, or an artist by color or form. She loved supremely, but she did not know that. She loved divinely, but her husband had never found it out. They were two plain people, a carpenter and his wife, plodding along the Connecticut valley industriously, with the ideals of their kind; to be true to their marriage vows, to be faithful to their children, to pay their debts, raise the tobacco, water the garden, drive the nails straight, and preserve the quinces. There were times when it occurred to Patience that she took more care of Reuben than Reuben did of her; but she dismissed the matter with a phrase common in her class, and covering for women most of the perplexity of married life: "You know what men are."

On the morning of which we speak, Reuben Oak had a blunt perception of the fact that it was kind in his wife to take such pains not to wake him till he got ready to begin the tremendous day before him; she always was considerate if he did not sleep well. He put down his hand and took hers with a sudden grasp, where it lay gentle and still beside him.

"Well, Peter," he said, kindly.

"Yes, dear," said Patience, instantly. "Feeling all right for to-day?"

"Fine," returned Reuben. "I don't know when I've felt so spry. I'll get right up 'n' dress."

"Would you mind staying where you are till I get your coffee heated?" asked Patience, eagerly. "You know how much stronger you always are if you wait for it. I'll have it on the heater in no time."

"I can't wait for coffee to-day," flashed Reuben. "I'm the best judge of what I need."

"Very well," said Patience, in a disappointed tone. For she had learned the final lesson of married life, not to oppose an obstinate man, for his own good. But she slipped into her wrapper and made the coffee, nevertheless. When she came back with it, Reuben was lying on the bed in his flannels, with a comforter over him; he looked pale, and held out his hand impatiently for the coffee.

His feverish eyes healed as he watched her moving about the room. He thought how young and pretty her neck was when she splashed the water on it.

"Goin' to wear your black dress?" he asked. "That's right. I'm glad you are. I'll get up pretty soon."

"I'll bring you all your clothes," she said. "Don't you get a mite tired. I'll move up everything for you. Your uniform's all cleaned and pressed. Don't you do a thing!"

She brushed her thick hair with upraised, girlish arms, and got out her black serge dress and a white tie. He lay and watched her thoughtfully.

"Peter," he said, unexpectedly, "how long is it since we was married?"

"Forty-nine years," answered Patience, promptly. "Fifty, come next September."

"What a little creatur' you were, Peter, just a slip of a girl! And how you did take hold - Tommy and everything."

"I was 'most twenty," observed Patience, with dignity.

"You made a powerful good stepmother all the same," mused Reuben. "You did love Tommy, to beat all."

"I was fond of Tommy," answered Patience, quietly. "He was a nice little fellow."

"And then there was the baby, Peter. Pity we lost the baby! I guess you took that harder 'n I did, Peter."

Patience made no reply.

"She was so dreadful young, Peter. I can't seem to remember how she looked. Can you? Pity she didn't live! You'd 'a' liked a daughter round the house, wouldn't you, Peter? Say, Peter, we've gone through a good deal, haven't we, you 'n' me? The war 'n' all that, and the two children. But there's one thing, Peter -"

Patience came over to him quietly, and sat down on the side of the bed. She was half dressed, and her still beautiful arms went around him.

"You'll tire yourself all out thinking, Reuben. You won't be able to decorate anybody if you ain't careful."

"What I was goin' to say was this," persisted Reuben. "I've always had you, Peter. And you've had me. I don't count so much, but I'm powerful fond of you, Peter. You're all I've got. Seems as if I couldn't set enough by you, somehow or nuther."

The old man hid his face upon her soft neck.

"There, there, dear!" said Patience.

"It must be kinder hard, Peter, not to like your wife. Or maybe she mightn't like him. Sho! I don't think I could stand that.... Peter?"

"Don't you think you'd better be getting dressed, Reuben? The procession's going to start pretty early. Folks are moving up and down the street. Everybody's got flowers. See?"

Reuben looked out of the window and over the pansy-bed with brilliant, dry eyes. His wife could see that he was keeping back the thing that he thought most about. She had avoided and evaded the subject as long as she could. She felt now that it must be met, and yet she parleyed with it. She hurried his breakfast and brought the tray to him. He ate because she asked him to, but his hands shook. It seemed as if he clung wilfully to the old topic, escaping the new as long as he could, to ramble on.

"You've been a dreadfully amiable wife, Peter. I don't believe I could have got along with any other kind of woman."

"I didn't used to be amiable, Reuben. I wasn't born so. I used to take things hard. Don't you remember?"

But Reuben shook his head.

"No, I don't. I can't seem to think of any time you wasn't that way. Sho! How'd you get to be so, then, I'd like to know?"

"Oh, just by loving, I guess," said Patience Oak.

"We've marched along together a good while," answered the old man, brokenly.

Unexpectedly he held out his hand, and she grasped it; his was cold and weak; but hers was warm and strong. In a dull way the divination came to him, if one may speak of a dull divination, that she had always been the strength and the warmth of his life. Suddenly it seemed to him a very long life. Now it was as if he forced himself to speak, as he would have charged at Fredericksburg. He felt as if he were climbing against breastworks when he said:

"I was the oldest of them all, Peter. And I was sickest, too. They all expected to come an' decorate me to-day." Patience nodded, without a word. She knew when her husband must do all the talking; she had found that out early in their married life. "I wouldn't of believed it, Peter; would you? Old Mr. Succor had such good health. Who'd thought he'd tumble down the cellar stairs? If Mis' Succor 'd be'n like you, Peter, he wouldn't had the chance to tumble: I never would of thought of David Swing's havin' pneumonia, would you, Peter? Why, in '62 he slept onto the ground in peltin', drenchin' storms an' never sneezed. He was powerful well 'n' tough, David was. And Jabez! Poor old Jabez Trent! I liked him the best of the lot, Peter. Didn't you? He was sorry for me when they come here that day an' I couldn't march along of them.... And now, Peter, I've got to go an' decorate them.

"I'm the last livin' survivor of the Charles Darlington Post," added the veteran. "I'm going to apply to the Department Commander to let me keep it up. I guess I can manage someways. I won't be disbanded. Let 'em disband me if they can! I'd like to see 'em do it. Peter? Peter!"

"I'll help you into your uniform," said Patience. "It's all brushed and nice for you."

She got him to his swaying feet, and dressed him, and the two went to the window that looked upon the flowers. The garden blurred yellow and white and purple, a dash of blood-red among the late tulips. Patience had plucked and picked for Memorial Day, she had gathered and given, and yet she could not strip her garden. She looked at it lovingly. She felt as if she stood in pansy lights and iris air.

"Peter," said the veteran, hoarsely, "they're all gone, my girl. Everybody's gone but you. You're the only comrade I've got left, Peter.... And, Peter, I want to tell you, I seem to understand it this morning. Peter, you're the best comrade of 'em all."

"That's worth it," said Patience, in a strange tone, "that's worth the high cost of living."

She lifted her head. She had an exalted look. The thoughtful pansies seemed to turn their faces toward her. She felt that they understood her. Did it matter whether Reuben understood her or not? It occurred to her that it was not so important, after all, whether a man understood his wife, if he only loved her. Women fussed too much, she thought; they expected to cry away the everlasting differences between the husband and the wife. If you loved a man you must take him as he was, just man. You couldn't make him over. You must make up your mind to that. Better, oh, better a hundred times to endure, to suffer, if it came to suffering, to take your share (perhaps he had his, who knew?) of the loneliness of living. Better any fate than to battle with the man you love, for what he did not give or could not give. Better anything than to stand in the pansy light, married fifty years, and not have made your husband happy.

"I 'most wisht you could march along of me," muttered Reuben Oak. "But you ain't a veteran."

"I don't know about that," Patience shook her head, smiling, but it was a sober smile.

"Tommy can't march," added Reuben. "He ain't here; nor he ain't in the graveyard either. He's a ghost, Tommy. He must be flying around the Throne. There's only one other person I'd like to have go along of me. That's my old dog, my dog Tramp. That dog thought a sight of me. The United States army couldn't have kep' him away from me. But Tramp's dead. He was a pretty old dog. I can't remember which died first, him or the baby; can you? Lord! I suppose Tramp's a ghost, too, a dog ghost, trottin' after, I don't know when I've thought of Tramp before. Where's he buried, Peter? Oh yes, come to think, he's under the big chestnut. Wonder we never decorated him, Peter."

"I have," confessed Patience. "I've done it quite a number of times. Reuben? Listen! I guess we've got to hurry. Seems to me I hear -"

"You hear drums," interrupted the old soldier. Suddenly he flared like lightwood on a camp-fire, and before his wife could speak again he had blazed out of the house.

The day had a certain unearthly beauty, most of our Memorial Days do have. Sometimes they scorch a little, and the processions wilt and lag. But this one, as we remember, had the climate of a happier world and the temperature of a day created for marching men, old soldiers who had left their youth and strength behind them, and who were feebler than they knew.

The Connecticut valley is not an emotional part of the map, but the town was alight with a suppressed feeling, intense, and hitherto unknown to the citizens. They were graver than they usually were on the national anniversary which had come to mean remembrance for the old and indifference for the young. There was no baseball in the village that day. The boys joined the procession soberly. The crowd was large but thoughtful. It had collected chiefly outside of the Post hall, where four old soldiers had valiantly sustained their dying organization for now two or three astonishing years.

The band was outside, below the steps; it played the "Star-spangled Banner" and "John Brown's Body" while it waited. For some reason there was a delay in the ceremonies. It was rumored that the chaplain had not come. Then it went about that he had been summoned to a funeral, and would meet the procession at the churchyard. The chaplain was the pastor of the Congregational Church. The regimental chaplain, he who used to pray for the dying boys after battle, had joined the vanished veterans long ago. The band struck up "My Country, 'tis of Thee." The crowd began to press toward the steps of the Post hall and to sway to and fro restlessly.

Then slowly there emerged from the hall, and firmly descended the steps, the Charles Darlington Post of the Grand Army of the Republic. People held their breaths, and some sobbed. They were not all women, either.

Erect, with fiery eyes, with haughty head, shrunken in his old uniform, but carrying it proudly, one old man walked out. The crowd parted for him, and he looked neither to the right nor to the left, but fell into the military step and began to march. In his aged arms he carried the flags of the Post. The military band preceded him, softly playing "Mine Eyes have Seen the Glory," while the crowd formed into procession and followed him. From the whole countryside people had assembled, and the throng was considerable.

They came out into the street and turned toward the churchyard, the old soldier marching alone. They had begged him to ride, though the distance was small. But he had obstinately refused.

"This Post has always marched," he had replied.

Except for the military music and the sound of moving feet or wheels, the street was perfectly still. No person spoke to any other. The veteran marched with proud step. His gray head was high. Once he was seen to put the flag of his company to his lips. A little behind him the procession had instinctively fallen back and left a certain space. One could not help the feeling that this was occupied. But they who filled it, if such there had been, were invisible to the eye of the body. And the eyes of the soul are not possessed by all men.

Now, the distance, as we have said, was short, and the old soldier was so exalted that it had not occurred to him that he could be fatigued. It was an astonishing sensation to him when he found himself unexpectedly faint.

Patience Oak, for some reasons of her own hardly clear to herself, did not join the procession. She chose to walk abreast of it, at the side, as near as possible, without offense to the ceremonies, to the solitary figure of her husband. She was pacing through the grass, at the edge of the sidewalk, falling as well as she could into the military step. In her plain, old-fashioned black dress, with the fleck of white at her throat, she had a statuesque, unmodern look. Her fine features were charged with that emotion which any expression would have weakened. Her arms were heaped with flowers, bouquets and baskets and sprays: spiraea, lilacs, flowering almond, peonies, pansies, all the glory of her garden that opening summer returned to her care and tenderness. She was tender with everything, a man, a child, an animal, a flower. Everything blossomed for her, and rested in her, and yearned toward her. The emotion of the day and of the hour seemed incarnate in her. She embodied in her strong and sweet personality all that blundering man has wrought on tormented woman by the savagery of war. She remembered what she had suffered, a young, incredulous creature, on the margin of life, avid of happiness, believing in joy, and drowning in her love for that one man, her husband. She thought of the slow news after slaughtering battles, how she waited for the laggard paper in the country town; she remembered that she dared not read the head-lines when she got them, but dropped, choking and praying God to spare her, before she glanced. Even now she could feel the wet paper against her raining cheek. Then her heart leaped back, and she thought of the day when he marched away, his arms, his lips, his groans. She remembered what the dregs of desolation were, and mortal fear of unknown fate; the rack of the imagination; and inquisition of the nerve, the pangs that no man-soldier of them all could understand. "It comes on women, war," she thought.

Now, as she was stepping aside to avoid crushing some young white clover-blossoms in the grass where she was walking, she looked up and wondered if she were going blind, or if her mind were giving way.

The vacant space behind the solitary veteran trembled and palpitated before her vision, as if it had been peopled. By what? By whom? Patience was no occultist. She had never seen an apparition in her life. She felt that if she had not lacked a mysterious, unknown gift, she should have seen spirits, as men marching, now. But she did not see them. She was aware of a tremulous, nebulous struggle in the empty air, as of figures that did not form, or of sights from which her eyes were holden. Ah, what? She gasped for the wonder of it. Who was it, that followed the veteran, with the dumb, delighted fidelity that one race only knows of all created? For a wild instant this sane and sensible woman could have taken oath that Reuben Oak was accompanied on his march by his old dog, his dead dog, Tramp. If it had been Tommy. Or if it had been Jabez Trent. And where were they who had gone into the throat of death with him at Antietam, at Bull Run, at Fair Oaks, at Malvern Hill? But there limped along behind Reuben only an old, forgotten dog.

This quaint delusion (if delusion we must call it) aroused her attention, which had wavered from her husband, and concentrated it upon him afresh. Suddenly she saw him stagger.

A dozen persons started, but the wife sprang and reached him first. As she did this, the ghost dog vanished from before her. Only Reuben was there, marching alone, with the unpeopled space between him and the procession.

"Leave go of me!" he gasped. Patience quietly grasped him by the arm, and fell into step beside him. In her heart she was terrified. She was something of a reader in her way, and she thought of magazine stories where the veterans died upon Memorial Day.

"I'll march to decorate the Post, and Tommy, if I drop dead for it!" panted Reuben Oak.

"Then I shall march beside you," answered Patience.

"What 'll folks say?" cried the old soldier, in real anguish.

"They'll say I'm where I belong. Reuben! Reuben! I've earned the right to."

He contended no more, but yielded to her, in fact, gladly, for he felt too weak to stand alone. Inspiring him, and supporting him, and yet seeming (such was the sweet womanliness of her) to lean on him, Patience marched with him before the people; and these saw her through blurred eyes, and their hearts saluted her. With every step she felt that he strengthened. She was conscious of endowing him with her own vitality, as she sometimes did, in her own way, the love way, the wife way, powerfully and mysteriously.

So the veteran and his wife came on together to the cemetery, with the flags and the flowers. Nor was there a man or a woman in the throng who would have separated these comrades.

In the churchyard it was pleasant and expectant. The morning was cool, and the sun climbed gently. Not a flower had wilted; they looked as if they had been planted and were growing on the graves. When they had come to these, Patience Oak held back. She would not take from the old soldier his precious right. She did not offer to help him "decorate" anybody. His trembling mechanic's fingers clutched at the flowers as if he had been handling shot or nails. His breath came short. She watched him anxiously; she was still thinking of those stories she had read.

"Hadn't you better sit down on some monument and rest?" she whispered. But he paid no attention to her, and crawled from mound to mound. She perceived that it was his will to leave the new-made graves until the others had been remembered. Then he tottered across the cemetery with the flowers that he had saved for David Swing and old Mr. Succor and Jabez Trent, and the cheeks of the Charles Darlington Post were wet. Last of all he "decorated Tommy."

The air ached with the military dirge, and the voice of the chaplain faltered when he prayed. The veteran was aware that some persons in the crowd were sobbing. But his own eyes had now grown dry, and burned deep in their sunken sockets. As his sacred task drew to its end he grew remote, elate, and solemn. It was as if he were transfigured before his neighbors into something strange and holy. A village carpenter? A Connecticut tobacco-planter? Rather, say, the glory of the nation, the guardian of a great trust, proudly carried and honored to its end.

Taps were sounding over the old graves and the new, when the veteran slowly sank to one knee and toppled over. Patience, when she got her arms about him, saw that he had fallen across the mound where he had decorated Tommy with her white lilacs. Beyond lay the baby, small and still. The wife sat down on the little grave and drew the old man's head upon her lap. She thought of those Memorial Day stories with a deadly sinking at her heart. But it was a strong heart, all woman and all love.

"You shall not die!" she said.

She gathered him and poured her powerful being upon him, breath, warmth, will, prayer, who could say what it was? She felt as if she took hold of tremendous, unseen forces and moved them by unknown powers.

"Live!" she whispered. "Live!"

Some one called for a doctor, and she assented. But to her own soul she said:

"What's a doctor?"

The flags had fallen from his arms at last; he had clung to them till now. The chaplain reverently lifted them and laid them at his feet.

Once his white lips moved, and the people hushed to hear what outburst of patriotism would issue from them, what tribute to the cause that he had fought for, what final apostrophe to his country or his flag.

"Peter?" he called, feebly. "Peter!"

But Patience had said he should not die. And Patience knew. Had not she always known what he should do, or what he could? He lay upon his bed peacefully when, with tears and smiles, in reverence and in wonder, they had brought him home, and the flags of the Post, too. By a gesture he had asked to have these hung upon the foot-board of his bed.

He turned his head upon his pillow and watched his wife with wide, reflecting eyes. It was a long time before she would let him talk; in fact, the May afternoon was slanting to dusk before he tried to cross her tender will about that matter. When he did, it was to say only this:

"Peter? I was goin' to decorate the baby. I meant to when I took that turn."

Patience nodded.

"It's all done, Reuben."

"And, Peter? I've had the queerest notions about my old dog Tramp to-day. I wonder if there's a johnnyquil left to decorate him?"

"I'll go and see," said Patience. But when she had come back he had forgotten Tramp and the johnnyquil.

"Peter," he muttered, "this has been a great day." He gazed solemnly at the flags.

Patience regarded him poignantly. With a stricture at the heart she thought:

"He has grown old fast since yesterday." Then joyously the elderly wife cried out upon herself: "But I am young! He shall have all my youth. I've got enough for two, and strength!"

She crept beside him and laid her warm cheek to his.

www.ingramcontent.com/pod-product-compliance
Lightning Source LLC
Chambersburg PA
CBHW061507040426
42450CB00008B/1513